GOLF SENSE

vs. COMMON-SENSE

A GUIDE TO BETTER GOLF.

GW00656663

Dr. JOHN O' LEARY.

Moanroe Press

Published in 2003 by
Moanroe Press,
Mullins Cross,
Ladysbridge,
Co. Cork,
Republic of Ireland.
Contact: moanroepressltd@Yahoo.ie

ISBN No.:0-9546204-0-2

Printed and bound in Ireland by Litho Press,
Midleton, Co. Cork.

CONTENTS

ACKNOWLEDGEMENTS

This book could not have come to fruition without the advice and assistance of several people. I wish to acknowledge my gratitude to Dermot Gileece whom I first contacted about the feasibility of the concept of the book some years ago. Dermot kindly read several drafts, offered constructive advice and encouraged me to continue with the work. Others who read subsequent drafts are too numerous to mention and I thank them sincerely for their time and effort. I would also like to thank Bill O' Callaghan of Litho Press for his astute advise and for allowing me to work on-site with the book. Bill is a true gentleman who freely offered help and assistance at all times. Thanks also to Alice and Cathy at Litho Press for their patience and help. I would also like to thank Siobhain O' Callaghan and Noreen O' Connor for their photographic input and analysis and Maeve O' Keefe for her illustrations/drawings.

The book is dedicated to those I hold dearest and who have given me so much - my parents Hugh and Nora and to my wife, Julie, and our sons Conor, Kian and Stephen.

Enquiries:

Contact: moanroepressltd@Yahoo.ie
                  087-6694086

maeveokeeffe@Hotmail.com (illustrations)

GOLF SENSE Vs. COMMON SENSE

INTRODUCTION:

This book describes how the typical naïve golfer often fails to move the golf ball properly on account of a particular approach to the task. *These golfers literally hit the ball with the clubs with their own physical force/strength.*

It is quite understandable that many naive golfers employ this particular approach to moving the ball since one moves the ball in other non-golf sports by using one's own force to do so. Furthermore, one uses one's common-sense to move objects in everyday life. It therefore seems logical to the naive golfer to use every club as a "hitting" instrument with which to beat the ball forward by personal strength or force. But golfers often encounter difficulties in moving the ball accurately to their targets by employing the clubs in this way, especially with the longer clubs.

What these golfers may not realise is that the design of the golf clubs is compatible to the natural swinging motion of every club. In these circumstances, they might consider the strategy of *moving the golf ball through the natural swinging motion of the clubs instead.* The aim of this book, then, is to describe how the natural golf swing - **golf sense** - may be a more reliable method of moving the ball rather than hitting it with the clubs with one's own force - **common sense.**

METHODOLOGY

The key methodology of this book is to get the reader to discover the natural golf swing as much as possible for themselves. It is vital, therefore, that the reader participates in a series of practise-swinging sessions so that they can initially create the natural golf swing almost unwittingly, as it were. Then once they are made aware of it, they can be guided to understand its various

1

components and replicate it for real on the golf course. The reader should participate in these practise-sessions in certain ways.

First, they should grip the clubs in such a way that it facilitates the *swinging* movement of the clubs. *The grip is the single most important aspect in creating the natural golf swing properly.* For now, all the reader needs to know is that they should hold the clubs primarily with the *fingers* when swinging the clubs in the practise-swinging sessions as distinct from the grip on the clubs with the *palms* of their hands. This aspect is described in more detail in forthcoming pages and in Chapter 4.

Now that the reader should hopefully be giving the clubs a greater opportunity to swing freely with a facilitating grip, they should next direct the swinging motions themselves in particular flight paths around the body. The desired flight paths that the clubs should take around the golfer's person are those that are taken when the clubs are simply swung around the upper body for swinging sake alone. These flight paths should then become natural to the physical characteristics of the golfer themself as long as the golfer's upper body remains stable throughout. Thus, the reader should create a natural golf swing unique to themselves.

It is vital therefore, that the participant strives to keep the upper-body stable when swinging the clubs in the earlier practise-swinging sessions. The participant will hopefully begin to understand why this has to be the case as they read on in the book.

It is easiest for the reader to create the natural golf swing with the eyes closed as they swing the clubs in the practise-swinging sessions. This should give the clubs a greater opportunity of being swung for the sake of swinging them only. After all, the reader should then have no other intention or motive to employ the clubs in any other way. And the reader should be in an ideal position to hone their senses to discern the particular characteristics of the natural swing when their eyes are closed.

Finally, the participant should ensure that they begin the swing in a particular way so that the swing can become a natural *golf* swing. The clubheads of the clubs will be resting on the ground at address before they attempt to swing the clubs. The participant should gently push the clubheads back along the ground until such time as they eventually leave the ground. They should then take particular flight paths around the participant's person to differing degrees as the upper body remains stable. The initiation of the swing is very important to creating the natural swing: if the clubhead does not enter its natural flight path at the beginning it is hardly likely to re-enter it at any point thereafter. Ideally the clubhead should be in its natural flight path when impacting the ball. The relevance of the initiation of the swing will be described in forthcoming pages.

The reader is guided to discover one characteristic of the natural golf swing after another and the author explains the reasoning behind each characteristic in turn. The author also offers the reader a variety of self-discovery exercises to help the reader to understand the nature of natural swinging motion and how it relates to the natural golf swing.

It should be noted that this book uses several analogies in describing how the natural golf swing functions. These analogies are analogies only. They are given without any scientific substance or correlation as to how the natural golf swing works. This book purposefully avoids scientific analyses of any kind since they might detract the reader from understanding the simplicity of the natural swing.

This book, instead, relies on observational science. Participation in the practice-swinging sessions should show the reader for themselves the characteristics of the natural golf swing. And hopefully the reader will come to understand the natural golf swing and be struck by its simplicity and accessibility such that they may be inspired with confidence to create it successfully.

WRITING STYLE

The core lessons of this book are transmitted in the first three chapters. Since a significant portion of the target audience may be new to golf, the author employs a somewhat didactic (teaching) and repetitive writing style in explaining these lessons. The remaining chapters deal primarily with the notion of the change of mindset. This subject is communicated through a more relaxed, conversational writing style more suited to the topic itself.

Practise-Swinging Session (correct take-away, finger-grip, stable upper-body and eyes closed).

CHAPTER 1: GOLF SENSE.

WHY THE NATURAL SWING IS A RELIABLE METHOD OF MOVING THE BALL IN GOLF:

SECTION 1: THE DESIGN OF THE GOLF CLUBS:

The design of the clubs incorporates several elements that apply distinct types of effects on the ball. In essence, the length of a club's shaft and its clubhead size and composition determines the amount of force the clubhead uses to move the ball forward. The loft of the clubface is a factor that moves the ball up into the air. Both elements combine in a series of ways to determine a specific distance and direction that the ball travels and takes with each individual club. And it is one combination in particular, that of loft being suited to shaft-length, that provides one of the frameworks for the overall theme of this book.

(i) The force that moves the ball forward:

One moves the golf ball forward by impacting it with the golf clubs. The golf clubs have different lengths of shaft so obviously the longer the club (shaft), the further the ball should move when it is impacted by the club. Golf clubs, therefore, have short, medium (known as "middle") and long shafts to move the ball short, medium and long distances.

The clubheads by which the clubs actually impact the ball also play a role in determining the distance the ball travels. The clubheads of the "irons" are similar in shape, size and weight. But the clubheads of the "woods" are bigger than those of the "irons". They consequently move the golf ball the furthest since they impact the ball with more momentum. Traditionally, these clubheads were heavier than those in the "irons". Nowadays their composition is generally of more solid mass and they are lighter in weight.

The golfer moves the ball by applying force to it with the clubs. The forces vary according to the amount of force used by the golfer, the length of club shaft and clubhead size and composition. The real question, however, is how does the golfer *employ* the force to move the ball? Many beginner/high-handicap golfers are keen to have this question answered since they encounter inconsistencies in moving the ball accurately with the clubs. And with the longer clubs in particular.

A golfer can, of course, employ a variety of techniques in employing the clubs to impact the ball with force to move it set distances. The underlying premise of this book, however, is that the typical naive golfer is more concerned with how much force is employed *onto* the ball to move it instead of how the force is employed *to* the ball to move it. These differences in approach should become apparent in due course. And they might resolve many beginner/high-handicap golfers' difficulties in moving the ball accurately.

But if shaft-length and clubhead size and composition are the factors that move the golf ball forward with the clubs, why should the clubfaces have different amounts of loft or "tilt"? After all, the clubs are designed by virtue of the factors above to move the ball forward a variety of distances so a player can send the ball to the pin whatever the distance. Well, not quite.

<u>(ii) The factor that moves the ball up into the air:</u>

Since the golf ball lies stationary on the ground it cannot be struck by a golf club from underneath to move it forward. This is the case in other ball games, for example, the lob in tennis. Neither can the golf ball be struck with great amounts of velocity from directly behind as in the case of a free kick in football. The footballer can run at the ball before kicking it but the golfer has to stand still to the ball as they employ the club. The only way the golf ball can be struck by a golf club to move it forward is by a descending/downward blow onto it (except in the case of the driver that requires an upward blow, see Chapter 4). And there is little point in striking the ball a downward blow if the face of the clubhead itself is blunt. It would be impossible in these circumstances for the ball to fly significantly up into the air. Thus,

Differing lofts

while the impact of the clubhead obviously forces the ball forward when it strikes the ball, the loft or "tilt" of the clubface sends the ball up into the air. And obviously, the higher or more tilted the clubface, the higher the ball is sent up into the air.

(iii) How the lofts allied to the shafts determine specific distances that the ball travels:

While the distance the ball travels varies significantly from 100 yards or so with a wedge to 250 yards or so with a driver the differences in length between the clubs themselves is relatively small. The length of the shaft of an eight-iron, for example, is approximately 91cm while a four-iron is approximately 96 cm. Thus, the actual differences in distances determined by the differences in the lengths of shafts alone would be quite small. So the clubs need another aspect to their design to make the differences in which the ball travels more meaningful.

This other aspect, of course, is the regulation of the loft of the club. Take, for example, a typical eight-iron club. When used properly this club should propel the ball between 140-150 yards. The shaft of the club is 91 cm long and its angle of loft in the clubface is 42 degrees. Imagine, if you will, the same club with the loft of a seven-iron (38 degrees). If this club was employed, the distance the ball would travel would be slightly greater than that of the standardised eight-iron. The power to move the ball forward is the same (same shaft-length) but the flight path would be slightly shallower (lower loft) so the ball would cover more distance through the air. But the standardised seven-iron has a shaft length of 93 cm which transfers greater power than the eight-iron. Thus, the combination of the seven-iron's greater length of shaft and lower loft results in the ball travelling a more meaningful distance than the eight-iron. Therefore, the lofts combine with the shafts to determine the individual specific meaningful distances that the ball travels with individual clubs.

Thus, shaft-length, clubhead size and composition and angle of loft primarily determine the distance a ball travels when impacted by a club. But distance is not everything in golf. It's time now to begin your first practice-swinging session to determine how these factors also combine to determine the direction the ball also takes.

SECTION 2: HOW DIFFERENT CLUBS TAKE DIFFERENT FLIGHT PATHS ONCE SWUNG NATURALLY:

Before the reader participates in the practice-swinging sessions, it is best to describe the importance of the correct take-away of the clubhead at the beginning of the swing and the importance of the finger grip to empower the clubs to swing since these are crucial to creating a natural golf swing properly.

THE IMPORTANCE OF THE CORRECT TAKE-AWAY:
The theory:
The reader is probably familiar with clocks that keep time accurately through the swinging of pendulums. When one purchases a pendulum clock, one begins the swinging motion of the pendulum by pushing it forward gently with the fingers/hand. The pendulum is securely attached to its origin of suspension by a rigid shaft and finds its own flight path. This will be in a steep arc in relation to its steep-angled origin of suspension.

The clubhead should also travel in a flight path in direct relation to its source of origin of suspension. At the beginning of the swing the source of origin of suspension of the clubs is the golfer's hands as they hold the clubs at address. When a golfer wishes to begin the swinging motion of a club, the club is not held directly from overhead as in the case of the pendulum but is angled according to how far away the golfer stands to the ball at address. The shorter the club, the nearer the golfer stands to the ball at address; the longer the club, the further back the golfer stands to the ball at address.

The clock-owner pushes the pendulum forward to begin its swinging motion and the pendulum begins to swing then in *its* natural flight path. So too, does the golfer push the clubhead back along the ground to begin its swinging motion. The ground acts as a runway, as it were, that the clubhead travels along before it enters its flight path around the golfer's body. *The length of the club's shaft dictates the amount of time the clubhead travels along the ground and the degree of arc the clubhead takes as it leaves the ground.* Thus, the clubhead enters a flight path that is consistent to that club's length of shaft i.e., the clubhead enters its *natural* flight path.

Once the golfer initiates the swinging motion of the club, the hands revolve around the golfer's body. Since the length of shaft itself remains constant, the resulting flight path should be consistent with the take-away (assuming the golfer's own physical characteristics remain constant, see section 3). Thus, if the clubhead enters its natural flight path at the beginning of the swing, it should continue to stay in its natural flight path as long as the golfer simply sustains the swinging motion to its natural cessation.

Therefore, if the clubhead was square to the ball at the beginning of the swing (at address), it should return to this position on the inverse of the beginning of the swing. This, of course, is the impacting of the ball. If the ball receives a square contact at impact by the clubhead, it should travel to its intended target. *This, in essence, is the beauty of the natural golf swing - its reliability in making square contact between ball and clubhead at impact.*

The reality:

The clubhead of a golf club, however, does not lie rigidly in suspension like the pendulum before it begins to swing. It lies rather as a lifeless, weighty object on the ground before the golfer. The weight of the clubhead, particularly that of a "wood" is such that the golfer has to employ physical strength (over and above that employed to initiate the swinging motion of a pendulum) to move it. Furthermore, the longer the club, the further the clubhead lies away from the golfer. Thus, the strain is greater in initiating the movement of the clubhead of that club as it lies on the ground before the golfer. And let's not forget that the clubhead is a "dead" weight and must be moved from inertia.

It is quite possible in these physically demanding circumstances that the golfer might not employ the correct amount of physical strength to begin the swinging motion properly. The golfer may not allow the length of shaft to dictate when the clubhead should leave the ground. They may employ too much physical strength and take the clubhead off the ground themself instead.

If this happens, the flight path the clubhead takes cannot be natural to the club's physical characteristics, namely, its length of shaft. It is unlikely that the clubhead will enter its natural flight path. This phenomenon is known as *"picking the clubhead off the ground"*.

Pushing the clubheads gently back along the ground at the beginning of the swing is the only conscious action a learner golfer should make when attempting to create the natural golf swing. This comes automatically after time and practice. It obviously takes more physical strength to initiate the movement of a longer club than a shorter club. But whatever the amount of physical strength uired, it should be applied gently.

Correct take-away

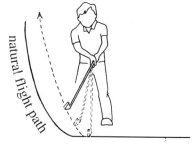

Incorrect take-away

The pendulum is securely attached to its origin of suspension by a rigid shaft as it begins its natural swinging motion. The golfer also keeps the hands and arms rigid as they begin the take-away of the clubheads. It's like a child on a swing-chair who asks their parent to push the swing-chair to begin its swinging  motion. Very often, the parent pushes the swing-chair too abruptly. The chair jerks sideways because the rope attaching the swing-chair to the crossbar flexes and bends. The swing-chair does not swing properly/in its natural flight path initially. If the parent pushes the swing-chair more gently, on the other hand, the rope should remain rigid and firm. The chair should enter its natural flight path and swing smoothly in it.

LESSON No. 1:

To begin the swing properly, the golfer keeps the hands and arms rigid and pushes the clubhead gently along the ground. The clubhead is allowed to take a path along the ground that is consistent with the turning of the golfer's wrists, arms, shoulders and upper-body. The length of shaft should then dictate the time it takes for the clubhead to leave the ground and consequently enter its natural flight path itself. Once the motion has begun, the arms and hands lose their rigidity as they rotate with the swinging motion of the club.

THE IMPORTANCE OF THE FINGER GRIP:

The grip golfers place on the clubs invariably reflects their intentions on how they wish to use the clubs to move the ball. After all, the grip is the only physical link between golfer and golf clubs to accomplish this task. A lot of golfers employ a tight grip on the clubs with the palms of the hands since it is their intention to hit the ball with the clubs with their own physical strength. This forceful action on the ball with the clubs requires such a firm, if not often over-powering, grip on the clubs.

But the golfer who wishes to create natural swinging motion with the clubs through which the ball can be moved has to employ a different grip on the clubs for several reasons. Firstly, this grip should be *flexible* enough to allow the clubs to swing around the body in the first place. Secondly, and closely related to this, the grip should be such so that the golfer is *restricted* from exerting any personal influence on the flight paths the clubs take. The answer to these prerequisites lies in the finger grip.

How the finger grip allows swinging motion to take place and restricts the golfer from exerting personal influence on the flight paths at the same time:

The finger grip cannot stifle the motions of the clubs as they are being swung since the golfer is not using the palms of the *hands* to personally direct the motions of the clubs. Think of the grip a jockey uses on the reins of his horse during a horse-race. He holds the reins with his fingers when he wants the horse to run as fast as he can. The hands and wrists remain limp. This "loose" finger grip gives the horse's head the freedom it requires for the horse to run as quickly as possible.

Yet when the jockey wishes to slow the horse down, he adopts a firmer grip with the palms of the hands on the reins to restrict the movement of the horse's head. The jockey is now dictating the movements of the horse by pulling back tightly on the reins with the palms of the hands through activating the wrists.

13

Similarly, if the golfer's grip was primarily with the palms of the hands it would likely restrict the swinging motions the clubs could take. When the golfer uses the hands to employ the clubs in their own way, the wrists usually dictate the motions the clubs take. The golfer's finger grip, on the other hand, gives the clubs the opportunity to swing. Even though the golfer rotates the hands, arms, shoulders and torso to swing the clubs, the wrists simply rotate in tandem with and follow the now more likely swinging motions of the clubs as they are taken around the golfer's person. But the golfer must keep the upper body stable so that the flight paths the clubheads take are natural to the golfer's physical characteristics (see Section 4).

The finger grip also facilitates the swinging motion of a club because it enhances the golfer's perception of the amount of strain it takes of them to swing the clubhead from its inception to its completion around the body.

You should see for yourself in the practice-swinging sessions how this strain varies from club to club. The amount of strain to swing the short club should be relatively small. The clubhead should lie a relatively short distance away from your hands as you swing it. The swing shape the clubhead should take should not be really *around* your body as such. The amount of

14

strain to swing the long club, on the other hand, should be significantly greater. Not alone is the clubhead lying further away from you as you swing it, if the club is a "wood" its clubhead is bigger than that of the short club. Furthermore, the swing shape the clubhead should take should be more *around* your body than that of the short club.

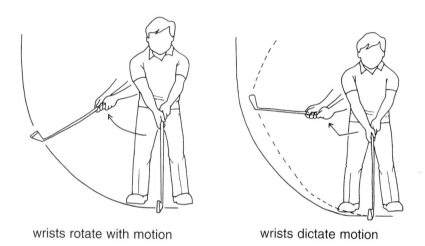

wrists rotate with motion   wrists dictate motion

The firmness of the finger grip:

The grip cannot be singularly flexible, however. The face of the clubhead may be square to the ball at address but it may not return square to the ball at impact if the clubhead is allowed to rotate too freely or too loosely as it is being swung. In other words, the finger grip should be firm so that the clubhead should not lose its angle of clubface (presumed to be square at address) as it is swinging around the golfer's body.

The grip itself should also be firm so that the impact between ball and clubhead will not loosen the grip from which the clubhead may not impact squarely through the ball. If the clubhead

15

is approaching the ball square before impact, the impact itself may twist the clubhead on impact or during impact if the grip is not firm enough. All the good work of getting the clubhead to return square to the ball would be undermined. So while the golfer holds the clubs primarily with the fingers, the fingers themselves must have a firm grip on the clubs.

DISCOVER FOR YOURSELF:

The finger grip gives the clubs the freedom to swing and gives power to the swinging motion itself. Grip a golf ball primarily with the fingers. Mimic a swing with your hand and release the ball as it is being swung. Then grip a golf ball primarily with the palms of your hands. Repeat the  swinging procedure. Which grip facilitated the swinging motion better? Which moved the ball further?

Palm-grip

Finger-grip

How to grip the clubs with your fingers:

Essentially one wraps the fingers around the handle of the club first and then places the thumbs on the handle of the clubs. The most common type of finger grip is whereby the index finger of the upper hand overlaps the small finger of the lower hand while

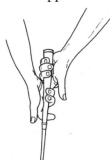 the index finger of the lower hand lies loosely around the handle of the club. This essentially leaves five fingers in control of the club - the two middle fingers of the lower (dominant) hand

16

and the last three of the other hand. The thumbs act more or less as stabilisers to the process (the Vardon grip).

Take note that while the fingers wrap around the handle of the club, the handle cannot but help rest against the palms when the golfer closes the hands. With the "palm" grip, however, the palms wrap around the handle as the hands are closed and the fingers have little influence on the grip itself.

The sensation of the finger grip may be awkard at first so practice and perseverance is the key. It actually does not matter how the fingers hold the club as long as they hold the clubhead firmly square at address so that the clubhead can be returned square to the ball at impact.

Thus, the finger grip is sensitive but firm and if you employ it in the practice-swinging sessions you are more likely to create swinging motion with the clubs. This, allied to a stable upper-body and a gentle take-away of the clubheads, should go a very long way to creating the natural golf swing.

THE PRACTISE-SWINGING SESSION:

The reader should now take out a short iron, for example, a pitching wedge, and place the clubhead on the ground as if to propel an imaginary golf ball. Remember to hold the club primarily with your fingers and not with the palms of your hands. Close your eyes to block out any thoughts other than swinging the clubs to ensure that the clubs will swing freely around your body. With your eyes closed, you should also be able to discern quite clearly the actual flight path the clubhead takes as you swing it.

Now begin the backswing. Keep your hands and arms rigid as you simply push the clubhead back gently along the ground. This is often referred to as taking the clubhead back in *"one-piece"*. The clubhead should eventually begin to take an arc path corresponding to the turning of arms, shoulders and upper-body and the natural cocking of your wrists as the club begins to revolve around your body. Keep your upper body stable.

17

The clubhead should not travel very far along the ground before leaving it and going up into the air. The top of the backswing is reached before the clubhead could have gone around the back of your body. Now begin the downswing. Do not influence the flight path of the clubhead in any way but simply allow it to go back along the flight path it had taken on the backswing. Thus, the flight path should remain consistent throughout. You should notice how the descent of the clubhead is again somewhat pronounced and how it comes down more onto the back of the (imaginary) ball. The club takes an inverse of the arc of the backswing on the follow-through. The shortness of the shafts means that the flight path or arc of the shorter clubs on the backswing, downswing and follow-through is rounded but not overly so.

Now take out a longer club, for example, a 4 iron or even better, a wood, and swing it naturally as described above. Adopt the finger grip and close your eyes. You should begin the backswing in the same way as you did with the short club so that the clubhead leaves the ground of its own accord, as it were. Keep your upper body stable.

This time you should note that the (long) clubhead spends more time travelling along the ground on the backswing before going into the air than did the clubhead of the shorter club. The (long) clubhead should have begun to travel well into an arc around your feet before ascending. The clubhead of the shorter club, on the other hand, should have taken its ascent as it had entered an arc around your feet. Furthermore, the ascent of the (long) clubhead into the air should have been gradual or stepped whereas the ascent of the clubhead of the shorter club should have been somewhat quicker and steeper. The top of the backswing is reached when the clubhead has gone around the back of your body.

Begin the downswing naturally, that is, do not influence the flight path the clubhead takes in any way so that it comes down along the path it took on the backswing. You are essentially swinging the club for the sake of swinging it only. You should note how the clubhead should have taken a more sweeping descent, more gradual and stepped, which placed the clubhead more *behind* the back of the (imaginary) ball before impact. The descent of the clubhead of the shorter club, on the other hand, should have been more *onto* the back of the ball. The club takes an inverse of the arc of the backswing on the follow-through. The longer length of the shafts of these clubs means that the flight path or arc of the longer clubs on the backswing, downswing and follow-through is more rounded and shallow that that of the shorter clubs.

It's likely, of course, that the participant may not discern these differences after a solitary swing of each club. Swing the clubs several times each and hopefully the differences should become apparent to you. These are, after all, *practise*-swinging sessions.

LESSON No. 2:

> **When swung naturally, the longer clubs have a more shallow (or "flatter") arc (or "plane") than the shorter ones and they go around the golfer's body more than the shorter clubs do.**

SHAPES OF DIFFERENT FLIGHT PATHS OF SHORT AND LONG CLUBS

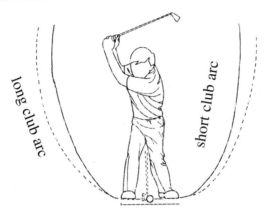

CORRECT & INCORRECT TAKE-AWAY

"Picking" the clubhead off the ground is like a situation whereby the runway controller in an airport knows that an airplane needs a certain length of runway to take off safely. They advise the pilot accordingly. But the pilot disregards this advise. They decide to attempt a take-away themself well before the actual length of runway should dictate. The result, of course, is disaster. Similar ill-effects with the long clubs will become apparent quite soon.

SECTION 3: THE SIGNIFICANCE OF DIFFERENT FLIGHT PATHS BEING TAKEN BY DIFFERENT CLUBS:

These differing flight paths of differing clubs bear three significant implications.

1.DIFFERENT FLIGHT PATHS DENOTE DIFFERENT AMOUNTS OF SWINGING MOTION:

The short club took a lesser rounded, more steep and shorter flight path "around" the golfer's person than did the long club. While there is swinging motion in every club, *there is more swinging motion associated with the long club than the short club.* We will see in due course how this factor is the central concept around which short, middle and long clubs work through natural swinging motion.

LESSON NO. 3:

> **The amount of swinging motion in a club increases as the shaft increases - thus, short clubs have certain amounts of swinging motion, middle clubs have more swinging motion whilst the longer clubs have most swinging motion.**

2.DIFFERENT FLIGHT PATHS DENOTE DIFFERENT ANGLES OF APPROACH:

The angle the clubhead of a short club takes as it approaches the ball on the downswing before impact is somewhat steep (known as the angle of approach). The ball itself receives a rather severe downward blow onto its back when the clubhead actually impacts with the ball. This type of downward blow reduces the loft of the clubface on the clubhead. This, in turn, reduces the chances that the ball can be propelled successfully up into the air because the greater/bigger the loft the better the clubhead is enabled to get the ball up into the air.

But the clubhead does indeed succeed because its designed loft is quite high anyway. The high loft of the short irons "forgive" the "choppy" blow onto the ball because the clubface still has a considerable amount of "tilt" left, as it were, upon contact with the ball. While there is a reduction in loft from the downward blow, there still remains sufficient loft in the clubface to get the ball up into the air successfully.

The clubhead of a longer club has a lower loft than that of a shorter club. It propels the ball longer distances by virtue of a lower flight path through the air as distinct from up into the air with the short clubs. The angle of approach is downward but not as downward as a short club. It places the clubhead more *behind the back of the ball* before impact rather than *onto the back of the ball* as in the case of the shorter club.

But since the loft of a long club is less than that of a shorter club, *it is better that it makes contact with the ball from an angle of approach that is more behind the ball.* If it makes contact with the ball from a more downward angle of approach as with a short iron there may not be enough loft left in the clubface to make proper contact at all. The downward blow could reduce an already low level of loft to a meaningless level. The ball could scuttle off sideways or move in a very low trajectory without little power since the contact between ball and clubhead could be stifled or "blocked". It would be like hitting the ball a downward blow with a sledgehammer!!! In other words, the loft of a long club has less "forgiveness" or compensation than a shorter club. An overly steep angle of approach could cause difficulties when moving the ball. This concept is explained in more detail in forthcoming pages.

In both cases, the angle of approach of the clubhead to the ball is different. But in each case it is the correct one for the respective loft of each clubhead from which the ball can receive an appropriate contact to send it on an appropriate flight path or direction. *In each case, the angle of approach of clubhead is the same as the angle of take-away of the clubhead at the beginning of the swing.* It's like how differing aircraft take-off from and approach a runway differently for a safe take-away and landing. A helicopter can take-off and land safely onto the runway through a more vertical angle akin to a short club. An airplane, on the other hand, needs to travel further along the runway and takes a more stepped, ascending take-off whilst its descent is more gradual for a safe landing akin to a long club.

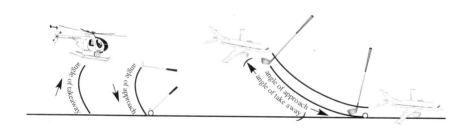

LESSON No. 4

3. DIFFERENT FLIGHT PATHS IMPART DIFFERENT TYPES OF SPIN ONTO THE BALL:

The lofts and lengths of shaft and the different flight paths different clubs take also combine to generate another force on the ball - the means by which the ball spins once it has been impacted by the clubhead. This factor is also instrumental to the direction and distance that the ball travels.

(i) the short irons cultivate backspin:

We have already established how the clubhead of a short iron impacts the back of the ball with a somewhat downward blow. The grooves of the clubface grip the ball upon impact so that it is dragged backwards along the clubface before being forced forward from the momentum of the overall force. The "choppy" impact forces the ball to revolve from bottom to top around as well as forward and imparts what is known as *backspin* on the ball.

Snooker players often use the backspin technique by stabbing or jabbing the cue tip down onto the back of the cue ball. When the cue ball strikes the first snooker ball in its line the cue ball literally screws backwards along the table to line up with its next intended potting opportunity.

Since backspin is encouraged by a steeper type of angle of approach it is most noticeable, then, in the short irons. It plays a significant role in determining the direction and distance that the golf ball takes when impacted by these clubs. Firstly, a golf ball is unlikely to bounce forward very far from where it lands on the ground due to the backspin exerted on it by a short club. After all, the ball is spinning backwards to some degree as it lands on the ground. Thus, when an average golfer uses a short iron, the ball is likely to come to rest near where it lands. The shorter the short iron, the greater the amount of backspin. Thus, the nearer the ball should come to rest from where it lands. Thus, backspin enables the short irons to be very accurate in terms of distance in relation to the pin (as long as one knows how far each short iron propels the ball).

Secondly, backspin influences the direction the ball takes. We read earlier how the ball's progress forward is hindered by backspin since the ball begins to revolve backwards as it moves forward. But this is a beneficial influence on the ball because the ball is more likely to go forward in a straight line since no other force other than forwards or backwards is being imparted on it. Whilst the ball's forward and backward motions affect the ball's overall forward motion, these motions effect a more or less straight flight path for the ball. Thus, short clubs – once used properly – are very accurate in terms of direction to the pin since there is every reason to believe (from physical circumstances at least) that the ball has a greater likelihood to travel in a straight flight path.

(ii) the long clubs cultivate sidespin:

We noted in Lesson No. 2 that the longer clubs go around the golfer's body more than the shorter clubs do. Thus, the downward action of a long club is accompanied by a more swinging motion. The clubhead is coming into the ball at impact from more *around* the *side* of the golfer's body rather than more from above as in the case of a short club. The loft of the clubface of a long club is much less than that of a short club. This reduced loft in the long club means that the ball has less scope or manoeuvrability to travel back along the clubface upon impact than would be the case of the clubface of a shorter club. The ball, if anything, is more likely to move *across* the clubface of a long club than back along it.

Think of moving sand with a shovel and a spade. The shovel has depth in its face so that when it is first dug into the sand, the sand should move back into the face of the shovel. Then as the shovel is moved forward to gather the sand, the sand should continue to travel back into the face and  then up along the face of the shovel. The shovel should gather a substantial amount of sand.

The spade, on the other hand, has little depth in its face. When it is first dug into the sand, the sand should move back into 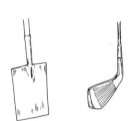 the face of the shovel. But as the spade is moved forward to gather the sand, the sand should not continue to travel back into the face because the face is too shallow. The sand consequently cannot move up along the face of the shovel but rather moves across the face of the spade. The spade should not gather as substantial an amount of sand as the shovel. The shovel was more beneficial to the person who used it to move the sand. The spade is better employed to cut slices of turf out of the ground.

The clubhead of a long club also approaches the ball from a downward angle. But it is a more shallow downward angle than that of a short club. We would expect some amount of backspin on the ball from the blow of a long club but it could never be as much as that inflicted by a short club. However, the combination of the clubhead approaching the ball from around the *side* of the golfer's body and the reduced manoeuvrability of the ball to travel back along the clubface results in the ball receiving a more dominant type of spin. It is more likely to be forced to spin sideways after impact. Just as the face of the spade can cut out slices of turf, so too can the face of a low-lofted club cut across the ball at impact and impart what is known as *sidespin*.

Snooker players also often use this sidespin concept by striking the cue tip into the side of the white ball. When the cue ball strikes the first snooker ball in its line the cue ball literally screws sideways away from the struck ball (left or right depending on which side the cue tip struck the white ball first). It then lines up with its next intended potting opportunity.

It is very important for naive golfers to be aware of the nature of this sidespin phenomenon. First and foremost, naive golfers should be comforted to know that physical characteristics simply make it more difficult to move a golf ball in a straight flight path with a long club than with a shorter club. Many, if not most, of the professional golfers incur sidespin to some small degree at times in their swing. Indeed, they often manipulate their address to the ball so as to cultivate it in their play (fades and draws). The "margin for error", as it were, is lesser with a long club than with a short club. After all, the clubhead is coming in to hit the ball from a sideways angle and the loft is not at all forgiving.

Secondly, sidespin is also used in other ball sports because the greater width of swing/strike is suited for long distance play when the ball is stationary. Rugby players, for example, who take long distance free kicks, do not run straight up to the ball to kick it. Instead, they walk back from the ball in an arc and run at the ball to kick it from this arc path.

Thirdly, while backspin can reduce the distance a ball travels, sidespin can add length to the distance the ball travels. When a golf ball with sidespin lands on the ground, the spin can propel the ball sideways but forward. The ideal sidespin to propel the ball forward is known as a draw. For a right-handed player, the ball should spin right-to-left and vice-versa for the left-handed golfer.

The most important thing to understand is that sidespin is not necessarily a bad symptom of your long club swinging actions as long as the ball flies sideways gently and still remains on the fairway or light rough. If, however, the ball flies sideways violently out of bounds, then your "swing" needs to be analysed. Chapter 2 offers various explanations for this phenonomen, some of which are related to an exaggeration of the amount of sidespin imparted to the ball. And remember – backspin and sidespin are *consequences* of swinging action on the ball. The golfer does not have to consciously attempt to impart these spins on the ball with the clubs since they arise from the swing itself.

LET PHYSICS TAKE ITS COURSE - ONCE THE CLUBS ARE SWUNG PROPERLY

Nothing is as important as understanding the different flight paths that different clubs take as they are swung naturally around the golfer's body. These flight paths are responsible for the differences in the angles of approach that different clubheads make to the golf ball before impacting with it. And let's not forget that the differing flight paths also impart different types of spin on the ball. But where do the different flight paths come from? *They come from the golfer who swings the clubs naturally so that the clubs enter and remain in their natural flight paths in the first place.*

Thus, some golfers do not concern themselves with the differences in club shaft. Nor the differences in loft. Nor the differences in flight paths the different clubs take. Nor the differing angles of approach the clubheads take before and during impacting with the ball. Nor the differing spins the ball takes with differing clubs.

No – some golfers simply swing each club in the same natural way that you hopefully have already done in the foregoing practice-swinging session. Because once one swings a club naturally, one activiates a certain amount of swinging motion, be it little, large or in-between, with that club that empowers the laws of physics to propel the ball properly with that club.

The entire point of this book is to show that the golfer does not use any kind of arbitrary swing or action when employing the clubs to move the ball. The purposes of the practise-swinging sessions is to show how different clubs manifest different amounts of swinging motion when swung naturally. So the golfer should give the clubs the particular amounts of swinging motion they require when playing golf. This makes **golf sense**.

The practise-swinging sessions should also inform the participant how the created swinging motion influences the golfer and ball in turn. So the golfer should cater for these influences when playing golf. This also makes **golf sense**. These are the two keystones upon which the natural golf swing are founded.

In a sentence - golf sense is based on respecting the different amounts of swinging motion different clubs exhibit when swung naturally!

You may have heard the expression *"let the club do the work"*. This is exactly what good golfers do. They swing the clubs naturally and let the club get on with all the work of moving the ball. There is no need for the golfer to get personally involved. There is no need to manipulate or physically manoeuvre the club. There is no need to dictate what the clubs should do. Just swing them as naturally as your body allows.

Indeed, we will see in the first three chapters how all of the relevant aspects of natural swinging motion that center on the different amounts of swinging motion associated with different clubs invariably fall into place naturally........once the golfer intends to swing the clubs naturally and takes a practise-swing or two with the clubs first. More anon.

Short club natural swing.

Long club natural swing-
note motion more shallow
than short club.

Short club natural swing -
has a certain amount of
swinging motion but does
not bring clubhead fully
around golfer's back.

Long club natural swing-
clubhead goes fully
behind golfer's back - has
more swinging motion
than short club.

SECTION 4: THE NATURAL SWING, THE STABLE BODY AND SWINGING THE CLUBS FOR THE SAKE OF SWINGING THEM ONLY:

We read earlier how the clubhead enters its natural flight path by virtue of a correct take-away that is consistent with the physical charcteristics of the club (its length of shaft). But the clubhead can only remain in this flight path if the golfer's own physical characteristics remain consistent as well. Therefore, once the clubhead has entered its natural flight path, the golfer should ensure that the upper body or torso remains stable throughout the swing thereafter. Otherwise the flight paths the clubs take could be distorted with or interfered with as a result.

Think of a painter on a ladder who uses a paint-roller to paint a wall. The painter paints the wall by pushing the roller up and down the wall. There may come a point when the painter might stretch to push the roller up to its uppermost. If he stretches too much, he might de-stabilise his body and the paint-roller may leave the face of the wall. He would not be painting the wall. In a similar vein, then, the golfer should keep the upper body stable to ensure the clubheads remain in their natural flight paths as they are taken around the golfer's person to completion.

Furthermore, the stable central axis acts as a pivot to the free-swinging clubheads as they revolve around it. The clubheads should be swinging freely around the body on account of the appropriate finger grip. But they need to be guided or they could swing in any haphazard fashion. Thus, the stabilty of the golfer's body acts as a fulchrum for these free moving clubheads. It essentially guides the clubheads to take a shape as dictated by the stability of the golfer's upper body itself.

And the pivotting gives a consistency to the amount of swinging motion each club takes since the clubs are once again receiving resistance from the golfer's body. It's like the ring-master in a circus who keeps the lions and tigers under control with his whip. So too, does the stability of the golfer's upper body

31

control and delineate the flight paths the clubs take as they go around the golfer's body.

It's not, of course, that the golfer's upper body or torso remains stationary itself in order to be stable as the clubs are swung. The torso has to rotate as the arms and shoulders turn as the clubs are being swung around the body. But the torso rotates on an even keel, as it were, as it turns with the swinging motion of the clubs. The torso will be tilting to some degree at address when using any club - the shorter the club, the more tilted the torso should be. What the torso should not do is to tilt or sway out of the parameters as set down by the address position as the clubs are being swung around it. If this happens, the clubs will most likely leave their natural flight paths.

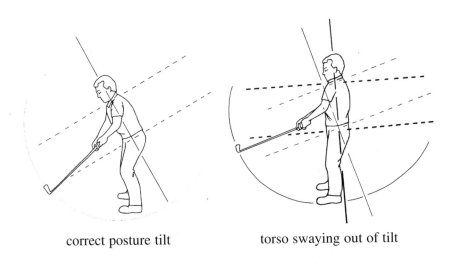

correct posture tilt   torso swaying out of tilt

When these consistencies occur, then, the resulting flight paths are essentially shaped by the golfer's own physical characteristics. They act as an uninterrupted or constant guide, as it were, for the paths the clubheads take as they *enter* and *go* "*around*" the golfer's person to *completion*.

This is known as the natural golf swing since the shape of

the swing becomes natural to the golfer's own physical characteristics. At its core, all the golfer has to do to create the natural golf swing is to simply swing the clubs freely and ensure that the body remains stable throughout so that the flight paths the clubs take should be shaped by and consistent to the golfer's body.

And come to think of it, isn't that what you did in the practise-swinging session earlier? You simply swung the clubs with no other intention in mind. The clubheads hopefully entered their own natural flight paths. You hopefully adhered to the advice to keep your upper body stable. The resulting flight paths of the clubheads hopefully remained consistent throughout until the swinging motion came to its natural cessation. Even though the flight paths were different with each club, each flight path was natural to each club. You created the natural golf swing with each club even though each natural swing had its individual characteristics.

Your overall physical stature or physique may be small, tall or somewhere in-between. You may have a particular rate of speed (rhythm) when doing things in everyday life and consequently when swinging the clubs. Generally speaking, the swing planes of a shorter golfer differ from those of a taller golfer when each swings the clubs naturally on account of these variations in individual physical tendencies/potential. Yet each swing plane and rhythm is relevant to the generation of a swing plane and rhythm that is natural to the golfer concerned. So each is equally effective despite the variations in individual physical characteristics.

When a golfer swings the clubs naturally, then, they ensure that the clubheads take the correct flight paths "around" *their* stable upper body. The clubheads, of course, also take their true flight paths when they are being swung for the sake of swinging them. In such instances, the golfer is doing nothing other than swinging the clubs and placing them in their true flight paths. *In other words, the golfer who intends to swing the clubs for swinging sake only - and uses only the physical energy required to do so only without de-*

stabilising the upper body - is essentially swinging the clubs naturally. Both concepts are intertwined and essentially mean the same thing.

And let's not forget that the correct amount of energy used to swing the clubs helps the golfer to maintain the stability of the upper body in the first place. What the golfer does not want to do is to employ *excess* energy to swing the clubs. This is likely to add further pressure on the golfer's upper body. That is likely to destabilise the upper body in its own right. And this might throw the clubheads out of their natural flight paths.

Thus, we have seen how the design of the clubs propels the ball specific distances and directions. The next question is how compatible is the natural swinging motion of golf clubs to the design of the golf clubs? And the reader may be forming an opinion on this matter already based on their experiences in the foregone practise-swinging sessions.

LESSON NO. 5:

> When a golf club is swung such that its clubhead enters and remains in a flight path to cessation without interference or distortion by the golfer, that flight path should remain consistent with the physical characteristics of that golfer. Thus, the clubhead should travel in a flight path that is natural to that golfer's physical characteristics. This is the natural swing.

SECTION 5: THE COMPATIBILITY OF THE NATURAL GOLF SWING TO THE DESIGN OF THE GOLF CLUBS:

ONE SWINGS THE CLUBS NATURALLY TO SEND THE BALL A SPECIFIC DIRECTION:

The contact between clubface and ball at impact determines the flight path of the ball after such impact. One assumes that before swinging the club at all that the clubhead is placed squarely behind the ball (the address position; see Chapter 4 "Pre-Swing Principles"). It can only make sense, then, that if the club is swung around the body without any interference to its flight path, the clubhead can only return to the position it took at address – square. If it impacts squarely with the ball, then, it should travel towards its intended target. This is a classic example of how **common sense** concurs with **golf sense.** So what's the problem? Well, the reality is that while **common sense** often concurs with **golf sense** in theory, it does not always concur with it in practice.

This, of course, is the natural swing. Essentially, the clubs are simply taken away on the backswing. They are brought back on the downswing and continued to the follow-through. The golfer does not influence their flight paths in any way. The golfer keeps the upper body stable as it rotates. The flight paths the clubs take are consequently shaped by the stability of the upper body. Thus, the clubs swing in their natural flight paths, be they somewhat steeper with shorter clubs or more shallow with longer ones. At its most basic, then, some golfers square the clubhead to the ball at address and *simply swing the clubs for swinging sake alone* to return the clubhead square to the ball at impact.

The reader should, however, take note of two very important points when attempting to return the clubhead square to the ball at impact. These, not surprisingly, relate to our understanding of the natural golf swing thus far.

Keep the central source stable:

A door that revolves around its hinges is another example of a natural swinging motion since its central source - the hinges - are screwed firmly into the door frame. When a door swings around its hinges, for example, it swings in a natural flight path from opening to closing and back again. Otherwise it could never be opened or closed properly. Thus, the door performs a natural swing in its own right because it revolves around a stable, central source. However, the motions a door takes when swinging naturally are often not the same as the motions golf clubs take when a golfer attempts to swing them naturally.

When a person closes a door gently the door closes properly. But very often people close doors aggressively and the doors still close properly...but only because the hinges of the doors are attached to strong wooden frames that can absorb the aggressive motions of the doors.

The golfer's central source around which the clubs are swung is the upper body/torso. The golfer can never be as physically a solid central source as a door frame to absorb abrupt, forced or aggressive action since the golfer relies on the stance to keep the torso stable. Abrupt or aggressive action on their behalf when employing the clubs can result in inconsistency in the motions of the clubs that could throw the clubheads out of their natural flight paths in its own right.

But abrupt or aggressive action on their behalf when "swinging" the clubs are more likely to de-stabilise the central source, the upper body/torso. If this happens, the clubheads are more likely to be thrown out of their natural flight paths. The swing, unlike the door swing, cannot then be a natural one. Indeed, another way of looking at it is that if the clubs are not in their natural flight paths, they cannot be receiving the amount of swinging motion they require. This makes **golfing sense**.

<u>Give the clubs the amount of swinging motion they require:</u>

We have already seen how each club's natural flight path brings about the correct angle of approach between clubhead and ball at impact to move the ball to the desired target. We saw earlier how there is lesser swinging motion associated with properly swung short clubs than longer clubs. *Effectively, short clubs do not really need to be swung naturally at all since they require little swinging motion anyway* (so abrupt/aggressive motions with shorter clubs may not be very harmful to their impacts to the ball, see Chapter 2).

On the other hand, swinging motion is certainly a more important characteristic of clubs other than the short ones, such as the mid-irons (7, 6 & 5) and most noticeably with the longest clubs (3, 4 iron & woods). *These clubs naturally take wide, shallow flight paths around the golfer's body that are, to all intents and purposes, significant swinging motions.*

And their lower-lofted clubheads require such amounts of swinging motion. They have to approach the ball from more behind the back of the ball to ensure enough loft is left in the clubfaces at impact. Thus, the golfer should swing these clubs naturally or else the angle of approach may be too steep. The subsequent  contact between ball and clubface at impact may not be suitable to move the ball to its intended target. This makes **golfing sense**.

Finally, it takes longer for clubs other than the short ones to complete their natural flight paths around the golfer's body because   these clubs have *more* swinging motion associated with them. The golfer who uses long clubs should give the clubheads the *time they require* to return square to the ball at impact. Swinging the clubs naturally gives the clubheads the appropriate amount of time they require to do so. But rushing or forcing the clubhead onto the ball may return the clubhead to the ball before it has had the time to be square at the point of impact - and may fail to move the ball accurately to its target yet again.

DISCOVER FOR YOURSELF

If you visit a children's playground you could observe how swing-chairs attached by longer ropes move more slowly that swing-chairs with shorter ropes. Ideally you should take hold of each swing-chair and let them go at the same time. You should notice that the chairs will remain in their natural flight paths as they swing and how the chair with the lesser rope

 comes back faster to you than the chair attached by the longer rope.

ONE SWINGS THE CLUBS NATURALLY TO SEND THE BALL SPECIFIC DISTANCES:
We read earlier in this chapter how the concepts of shaft-length, clubhead size/composition and angle of loft are responsible for the variance in power than can be transferred to the ball with different clubs. But another factor contributes to these variances in power. If you placed a short club in your hands, swung it "around" your body and released it, it would travel a particular short distance

away from you. If you replicated the same procedure with a longer club, it would travel a distance further away from you than did the shorter club.

The key concept, then, seems to be the effect of swinging motion on an object. Swinging an object around a central source seems to give power to that object. Once that object is released, the object travels a distance in relation to the distance the object was from the central source.

One example is the cowboy who uses a length of rope to lassoe a steed. The cowboy uses his body as a central axis for the rope as he swings it naturally around his body and above his head. The rope gathers and maintains momentum as it is being swung. When the cowboy releases the rope it hurtles forward – on account of the power that has been generated by the swinging motion of the rope - towards the steed and (hopefully) ends up around the steed's neck.

Similarly, the golfer should swing the golf clubs around a central axis - the golfer's body - to generate the power required to move the ball forward. But one does not release the golf club itself to move the ball. One releases the clubhead onto the ball instead. Remember: the clubhead, not the golfer, has the power to propel the ball forward because the swinging motion of the club generates the power that the clubhead, not the golfer, acquires. Thus, some golfers *allow the clubhead to impact with the ball as they swing the club around their person naturally until the swinging motion finishes.* This is one part of the second keystone underpinning the natural golf swing - how the swinging motion of a club influences the movement of the ball. If it is *allowed*, of course, to do so. This is **golf sense**.

The lack of awareness of how power is generated through the swinging of the golf clubs contributes greatly to the difficulties that some naive golfers endure when moving the golf ball. We will see in the following chapter how many naive golfers do not release the stored power of the clubhead onto the ball through the swinging motion of the club. They often physically imprison the clubhead themselves by using their own force or physical strength to hit the ball with the clubhead instead. And if you think about it, their action is quite understandable since it only makes **common-sense** that one should hit the ball with the clubs with one's own strength/ force to move it. After all, that is how we move the ball in other non-golf ball sports and objects in everyday life. **Golf Sense** Vs. **Common Sense.**

LESSON NO. 6:

The longer the shaft of a golf club, the more power is generated through the swinging motion of that club and the further the ball travels. Thus, golf clubs have short, medium and long shafts that can send the ball a variety of distances, short, medium and long, once they are employed properly. And the natural swing is one such means.

Do you not realise that you swung the clubs in this way in the practise-swinging session earlier? You generated *different amounts of swinging motion* with the clubs because they travelled in different flight paths. What are the flight paths of the clubs but indicators of the direction the clubs take as they swing around the body!

Thus, one does not have to hit the ball with the clubs with one's own personal force to move it particular distances. These actions, of course, are likely to be abrupt and/or aggressive on the ball with the clubs. Each club has a specific length of shaft and clubhead size/composition. These factors combined can determine a specific amount of power that can be generated onto the clubhead through the swinging motion of that shaft (club) around the golfer's body (to varying degrees). Short-shafted clubs send the ball a variety of short distances. Longer-shafted clubs send the ball a variety of longer distances. *On the assumption, of course, that they are swung naturally so that their clubheads move in their correct flight paths.* Then they can generate the correct amount of power from their swinging motions to move the ball.

Once one knows how far each club sends the ball on average, all one has to do is to rely on the principle of swinging the club naturally. The golfer lets the clubhead - which has acquired the power through the swinging motion of the club - to do the job of moving the ball. Once again, the expression *"let the club do the work"* comes into mind. Once again, hopefully, you understand why.

We have already seen how some naive golfers use abrupt/aggressive actions with the clubs on the ball. They often also fail to give the clubs the time they require to swing naturally. These actions can conspire not to move the ball accurately. Here we see how similar actions with the clubs can also conspire not to move the ball to desired, set distances. And in both cases, it is because the golfer is not giving the clubs the amount of swinging motion they require - the first keystone of the natural golf swing.

Thus, the principle of the natural swing is one means of generating the correct angle of approach between clubface and ball so that at impact it can send the ball onto its desired *direction*. And it is one means of generating the correct amount of force at impact to send it a desired *distance* as well.

LESSON No. 7:

The golfer might benefit from swinging each club naturally when attempting to propel the golf ball. This means that the golfer uses their energy to physically swing the clubs around the body only. They keep the body stable as it rotates throughout and do not exert any personal interference or influence on the path the clubhead takes as it goes around the golfer's body until the swinging motion is completed. In the process, the clubhead is allowed to impact the ball to move it to its intended target accurately, whatever its distance.

SECTION 6: CONCLUSION, RECAPITULATION AND PRACTISE-SWINGING SESSIONS AGAIN:

CONCLUSION:

In sum, then, the golf clubs have been designed such that the principle of the natural swing may be successfully applied to them to move the golf ball successfully. The situation with golf is like the every day experience of driving your car. When you start your car for a journey you don't have to worry about how the individual mechanical components of the engine combine to ignite and start. All you have to do is to turn the key in the ignition and the engine should automatically start. In essence, when you swing a club naturally, you give it the amount of swinging motion it requires to activate its inherent ability to propel the ball properly.

Technology nowadays has brought a change in the materials used in designing the clubs and golf ball. This serves the desire to propel the ball longer distances and to reduce the skill level required to move the ball properly. But buying an expensive club with graphite shaft and titanium clubhead does not exclude the need to employ that club properly. And the natural swing is one reliable means of doing so. What is the point in employing a top of the range driver that has the potential to move the ball huge distances if the method of employment of force is unreliable? What is the point in using a top of the range ball that has the potential to be moved huge distances if the method of employment of force is unreliable? In such circumstances, the ball will not travel to its intended target and will probably leave the golfer in serious trouble with the next shot.

Golf, then, can theoretically be viewed as a much easier game to play than other ball games. The simple, natural swing can become the foundation for every standard golf shot barring exceptions when the golfer literally has to beat the ball out of deep rough and so on. There are, of course, alternative strategies in using the clubs to move the ball. And there is more to moving the golf ball properly other than swinging the clubs naturally (these factors are described in Chapters 2, 3 & 4). But the simple fact of the matter is that the reader might consider that golf has its own logic and that the core of this logic is compatible with the natural golf swing.

YOUR NATURAL GOLF SWING:

The beauty of the golf swing is that it is unique to each individual golfer since it is created by each golfer's physical circumstances. While the principle and techniques of the natural swing are common to all, no two golfers can ever swing naturally the exact same way. Everyone has particular physical characteristics such as height, weight, length of arms, "elasticity" of turning body potential, upper and lower body strength and so on. People also approach life differently. Some are very casual and take their time in doing things. Others are anxious to do things as quickly as they can. And there is a multitude of degrees in-between.

No golf instruction book can make the reader swing the clubs with a rhythm and shape like that of a top-class golfer. This instruction book informs the reader of the importance of the natural golf swing, encourages the reader to discover its characteristics for themselves and offers guidance on techniques to help create it.

If the reader follows the tenets of this book and has the exact same physical characteristics of a top-class golfer, they could swing the clubs like that top-class golfer. If the reader follows the tenets of this book and adopts them according to their own physical characteristics it is likely that the reader will not swing like a top-class golfer. But there is no reason why the swing could not be as fundamentally and technically as sound as any top-class golfer's swing. And the swing will be yours, yours alone and yours for life whenever you require it as long as you swing the clubs naturally!

ACCESSIBILITY AND CORE CONCEPTS:

One component that does so much to bring about the correct flight paths is the *correct amount of energy* the golfer uses to swing the clubs in the first place. Using the correct amount of energy to swing the clubs naturally means that the clubs are being swung "around" the golfer's person at the correct speed or rhythm. This means the clubs are being given the amount of swinging motion they require by the golfer.

There are differences between the clubs themselves in terms of different lengths of shaft. The golfer should therefore take a practise-swing or two with each club to discern, amongst other things, the specific amount of energy required only to swing each individual club. This is exactly what the participant should have been doing in the *practise-swinging* sessions earlier.

And the task of identifying the correct yet differing amounts of energy to swing the different clubs should have been made a lot easier when the participant had their eyes closed during the practise-swings. Firstly, they should have been concentrating on nothing other than the swinging motions of the different clubs themselves. Secondly, they should have had no intention in mind other than swinging the clubs for swinging sake only. In such circumstances, the clubheads should have been swinging around the participant's person at very near to, if not the correct, rhythm in the first place. This is why the natural golf swing is so accessible.

The energy required to swing each club properly is but one component in creating the natural golf swing properly. Chapters 2 and 3 describe how other components are factored in. Everything comes from the intention to swing the clubs naturally in the first place followed by the discernment of the type of swinging motions created with the clubs thereafter in some practise-swings. It is through this process that the natural golf swing in its totality evolves. These are the core concepts of the natural golf swing. They identify the primary reasons why many golfers fail to move the ball properly with the longer clubs in particular. And the reader has already had a sneak preview as to how **golf sense** can often be in variance with **common sense**.

RETURN TO THE PRACTICE-SWINGING SESSIONS:
Swing the clubs again in another practise-swinging session. Can you confirm that the different clubheads do indeed take different flight paths "around" your body? Do you notice more swinging motion with the longer club than the shorter club? Do you notice that it takes more of your energy to swing the longer club than the short club? Although in both cases, the energy supplied by you is only the energy required to swing the clubs in the first place.

Unfortunately, one cannot determine whether or not the clubheads return square at the impact stage of the swing in the practise-swinging sessions. Why not go to the driving range and swing some clubs to find out? You can hardly create the natural swing there with your eyes closed. Try another technique instead.

Once you are ready to swing the clubs (assuming the clubheads are square to the ball at address), pick out a spot of ground an inch or so behind the ball. Focus on this spot of ground as you begin the swing, during the swing, when the clubhead impacts the ball and on the follow-through stage as best you can. Whatever you do, try not to observe the flight of the ball as soon as it leaves the clubface. Give this technique a chance. Concentrate on creating the natural swing only rather than on hitting the ball with the clubs. Allow the clubheads to impact the ball. Try it several times.

You may naturally be uncomfortable or sceptical when employing this technique at first. It might be beneficial if you ask a friend to observe whether the ball travels accurately to its intended target with short *and* long clubs. This should give you the ease of mind that you can impact the ball with the clubheads without having to look at the ball. It should also give you the confidence not to look at the flight of the ball as soon as it leaves the clubface. And you should not worry about losing the balls by not looking at them anyway since they are driving-range golf balls.

If your friend informs you that the balls do indeed fly off accurately, you can rest assured that the clubheads have indeed returned square to the ball at impact. Don't worry if the long clubs still offer inconsistencies as there are other factors to consider yet.

Whatever you do, do not concern yourself with *how far* you wish the balls to travel with the different clubs, the longer ones in particular. The entire premise of this book, you see, is that the typical naive golfer is probably pre-occupied with the power to move the ball long distances and that accuracy is affected as a result. *This book aims to correct this over-sight.*

Bear with this book until the end of Chapter 5 at least before you, too, become overly-focussed on employing force to move the ball. There is still a lot to discern and the power to move the ball should become apparent, slowly and discreetly, as the book unfolds.

And by the way, while you are on the driving-range, try and compare the amount of energy you use to swing the clubs with your eyes closed and when you swing for real to move some golf balls. Are there any differences, in particular, with how "forceful" you swing the long club with your eyes closed and when you employ it for real. Just something for you to start thinking about. Good luck!

RECAPITULATION:

(i) When swung naturally, longer clubs take wider and more shallow flight paths more around the body than shorter clubs do. Thus, there is more swinging motion associated with longer clubs than shorter clubs.

(ii) Swinging motion of the clubs generates power to move the ball within the clubheads.

(iii) Short clubs therefore generate little amounts of power that can only move the ball short distances. Longer clubs generate greater amounts of power to move the ball greater distances....when they are swung naturally.

The golfer should therefore avail of this power and swing the clubs naturally to move the ball distances relevant to the lengths of the shafts of the clubs and clubhead size/composition. The golfer could, of course, use alternative methods of employment of force to move the ball different distances on account of their standardised design.

But the golfer must also move the ball accurately to specific targets. The golfer might be better advised to swing the clubs naturally to achieve this because this is a reliable method of returning the clubhead square to the ball at impact - **golf sense.** And this is crucial for the longer clubs in particular.

(i) when longer clubs are swung naturally their clubfaces approach the ball suitably from a shallow and wide angle of approach. This is determined by their natural flight paths before impacting the ball. Any other angle of approach may fail to move the ball to its intended target because the low loft of the clubface may not be compatible to alternative angles of approach.

(ii) when longer clubs are swung naturally their clubfaces are given the amount of time it takes for them to rotate through their flight paths to return square to the ball upon impact with the ball (assuming square at address). Thus, the ball is sent to its intended target. Other usages of the long clubs may not give their clubfaces the time they require to return square at impact.

It seems a case could be argued for **golf sense** rather than **common sense.**

LESSON No. 8

In theory, the design of the golf clubs is compatible to the natural swinging of the clubs. In practice, however, shorter clubs do not necessarily have to be swung naturally since little swinging motion is associated with them. But the longer the shaft of a club, the more it requires swinging motion and greater is the need for such clubs to be swung naturally. For the sake of uniformity and to avoid confusion it's best to swing all the clubs naturally.

Long club natural sequence above; short club natural sequence below. Note smoothness of both arcs. Note completion of both arcs. Note long club arc wider than short club arc. Note backswing and follow-through of long club greater than that of short club signifying greater amounts of swinging motion around the golfer's body. Photographs on p.30 also show greater amounts of swinging motion in long clubs than short clubs.

CHAPTER 2: HOW COMMON-SENSE OFTEN HITS AND HOPES:

SECTION 1: OVERVIEW - HOW EXCESSIVE FORCE CAN AFFECT THE CONTACT BETWEEN BALL AND CLUBHEAD AT IMPACT.

The preceding chapter has described how the clubs can move the golf ball properly once they are swung naturally. Many naïve golfers focus on using the clubs to move the golf ball by hitting or beating the ball with the clubs with their own physical strength instead. Their wish, it seems, is to move the ball directly with the clubs themselves. This strategy is usually successful with the shorter clubs but it can be fraught with inconsistencies with the longer clubs. Chapters 2 and 3 seek to understand why this is the case.

It is very hard, of course, not to blame naïve golfers for approaching the task of moving the ball in their way. After all, in our everyday chores we constantly exert physical force ourselves on objects to move them. We often pull or push a door to open it, for example, or we shove a sweeping brush before us to tidy an area. Furthermore, many naïve golfers have had or continue to have previous other ball sport experiences, for example, football, tennis, squash/racquetball and so on. It's fair to say that many beginner golfers take up golf when they eventually retire from a physically more demanding ball sport. And isn't it by hitting or beating the ball with the striking equipment with one's own force that one moves the ball in other ball sports?

What compounds the situation is that the ball in the vast majority of other ball games is either bigger or heavier than that of the simple golf ball. Naïve golfers who have played such games are used to using considerable force to move the ball in these sports. Players literally have to hit or beat the

51

ball with their own strength in order to move it, either with some striking equipment or with their limbs! Therefore, it only makes **common sense** to many naïve golfers that they should literally force the clubhead *onto* the golf ball with their own physical strength to move the ball forward. And to do so quite forcibly if the distance the ball has to travel is quite significant. In fairness, the notion of moving the golf ball by swinging the clubs for swinging sake alone - **golf sense** - could sound ridiculous to them. It might seem either a too simplistic or too ineffective way of moving the golf ball, particularly with regard to significant distances.

<u>The differences in energy levels to create "swinging" action and "hitting" action:</u>

Swinging the clubs naturally literally means that some golfers use the energy it requires of them to swing the clubs *only and nothing else.* Such golfers use an amount of energy required only to initiate, sustain and complete the swinging motion of the club so that the clubhead remains in its natural flight path throughout. The golfer allows the clubhead to impact the ball through its swinging motion.

But golfers who attempt to hit or beat the ball with the clubhead with their own force/physical strength invariably use an amount of force *more* than that required to swing the club for swinging sake alone. When one swings a club naturally one is simply taking the strain of the weight of the clubhead at the end of the shaft and revolving this strain around one's body. When one uses "hitting" action on the ball with any club, one invariably uses one's own strength to *force* the clubhead onto the ball with the intention to move it.

LESSON NO. 9

The naive golfer should note the difference between using physical strength as an energy and using physical strength as a force. Some golfers use their physical strength as an energy to swing the club that in turn generates power onto the clubhead. These golfers then allow the clubhead to impart this power it has acquired onto the ball. The naive golfer, on the other hand, uses their physical strength as a force to move the golf ball by hitting the ball with the club with their own physical strength.

In a sense, it's as if when a naïve golfer were clay-pigeon shooting they would throw the rifle at the clay-pigeon with their own physical strength *to hit it*. Yet another golfer might use their physical strength to press the trigger and allow the bullet to do the work of *impacting* the clay-pigeon instead.

Naïve golfers may still be employing the force necessary to move the ball required distances with the clubs by using their own force/strength to do so. But it is the way they employ the clubs to impart this personal force that can become problematic since it is *their* force they are imparting. The amount of force is likely to be excessive since they are likely to hit the ball with the clubs with as much force as possible. We will see in this chapter how this *excessive* energy can create a lot of problems in terms of returning the clubhead square to the ball at impact. The errors that arise are primarily related to the *direction* the ball needs to be moved in.

And of course, this trend of using excessive force is commonplace in our everyday lives. We behave like this in an acceptable way both on and off non-golf sporting arenas. So we could easily become pre-conditioned into behaving in this way on the golf course as well.

SECTION 2: HOW THE CLUBHEADS OFTEN FAIL TO RETURN SQUARE TO THE BALL AT IMPACT:

ERROR NO. 1. THE EXCESSIVE SPEED THAT THE CLUBHEADS TRAVEL BEFORE IMPACTING THE BALL:

The differences in rhythms between "swinging" action & "hitting" action:

The clubhead that is swung naturally acquires a particular rhythm or rate of speed relevant to the flight path that particular clubhead takes as it goes "around" the golfer's body. Take out a short and long club again for your next practice-swinging session to discover this aspect of the natural golf swing. Hold the clubs appropriately, close your eyes, swing the clubs a few times and keep the upper body stable. Concentrate on the amount of time it takes for each club to complete its natural flight. Be sure to initiate the swinging motion properly in each case by gently pushing each clubhead back along the ground until each leaves the ground of their own accord, as it were. Thereafter simply sustain the swinging motions until they cease naturally on the follow-through.

Did you not notice how it took longer for the long club to complete its natural flight path around your body than it did the shorter club? This is because the long club had more swinging motion associated with it. It travelled in a wider flight path around your body than the shorter club did. *The rhythm of the shorter club was quicker than that of the longer club when both were swung naturally because essentially there was more swinging motion associated with the longer club than the shorter one.*

Yet despite the difference in their rhythms, both clubs were being swung at their *appropriate* rhythms. Thus, the golfer who swings any club naturally can rely on that clubhead returning square at impact with the ball whether its rhythm is quick, slow or any rate in-between (assuming square at address).

55

DISCOVER FOR YOURSELF:

Have you ever seen people/children playing a game called "swing-ball"? The ball is attached to a series of grooves on top of a pole. The players hit the ball with rackets/bats, one player moving the ball up the grooves, the other player moving the ball down the grooves. The winner is the one who reaches the top or the bottom of the grooves first. If the players were not competing against each other, they could simply play the game by hitting the ball with the bats and allow the ball to swing *around* the pole to each other. The ball would travel smoothly and slowly in this direction and the players could continue with the game with ease. The competitive nature of the game, however, means that the ball is often struck abruptly and aggressively so that at times it takes a more upward/downward motion. This, in turn, is harder for opponents to counter-act since the ball travels much quicker in such steep flight paths.

The situation with the naïve golfer is often different, however. We know now that the natural flight path the clubhead takes dictates the time it takes for the clubhead to impact the ball when the club is swung properly. This makes **golf sense**. But it is usually the naïve golfer's **common sense** *desire* to hit the ball with the club with their own strength that dictates the time it takes for the clubhead to impact the ball.

At the best of times, this desire is impulsive. All that matters to the naïve golfer is to move the ball by hitting it with the club with personal strength. Thus, they hit the ball with the club with indiscriminate personal force. At the worst of times, the naïve golfer hits the ball as hard as they can when using the longer clubs. Because they again use their **common sense** into believing *that the harder one hits the ball with the club, the further it travels.*

What the naïve golfer is doing, in effect, is bringing the clubheads of longer clubs onto the ball as quickly, if not more quickly, than the clubheads of shorter clubs. But we know now that the rhythm of a shorter club is quicker than that of a longer club when both are swung naturally. The clubhead of a longer club has to return to the ball from around the golfer's body on the downswing. By the time it impacts with the ball the clubhead will have revolved back to the point it held at address – square. When a naïve golfer hits the ball as hard as they can with a long club, they do not give its clubhead *the time it requires* or *enough time* to return square before it impacts the ball. **Golf Sense Vs. Common Sense.**

Thus, when a naïve golfer "hits" a ball with a long club with their own force, they invariably "swing" the club quicker than what its natural rhythm should have been. The likelihood is that the clubhead will return prematurely and not be square upon impact. The clubhead will probably return to what is known as an "open" position to the ball just before impacting it. The clubface will probably "cut across" the ball at impact and cause what is commonly regarded as a "slice".

Small amounts of sidespin can occur when impact

conditions are very good with long clubs. Flaws in impact conditions can only exaggerate the amount of sidespin imparted onto the ball. Thus, the glancing blow is likely to impart severe sidespin on the ball and

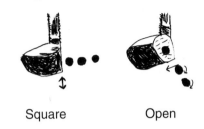

Square   Open

it is likely to veer away significantly from the intended target.

It's like a worker who takes a product off a conveyor belt to further process it. The conveyor belt runs at a particular speed so that the employee can safely handle the products and process them. If, however, the conveyor belt is speeded up, the employee will hardly be able to take the products safely off the conveyor belt......... let alone have the time to process them properly.

The dangers of using one's **common sense** in this way are lessened considerably when using the shorter clubs. Firstly, there is lesser rotation of the clubheads of properly swung shorter clubs than longer clubs. The clubheads of shorter clubs are not being moved *around* the golfer's body as much as in the case of the longer clubs. When a naïve golfer "hits" a ball with a short club with their own force quickly, the clubhead may not be revolving to any great degree during its flight path. Thus, there is a good likelihood that the clubhead will return square to the ball at impact. Secondly, the natural rhythm of short clubs is quick since there is little swinging motion associated with these clubs. And the typical "hitting" action on the ball is carried out quickly similarly.

In effect, then, the naïve golfer who uses their **common sense** and attempts to hit or beat the ball with a club with personal strength is relying on chance. The chance is whether or not the clubhead will return naturally at impact with the ball to the position it occupied at address (square). The chances of success are directly related to the length of shaft of club used: the shorter the club, the greater the chance of success, the longer the club, the lesser the chance of success. And the naive golfer probably does not realise that they are in a lottery!

Is the reader beginning to understand the significance of how different clubs exhibit different amounts of swinging motion when swung naturally? And how important it is for the golfer to **respect** these differing amounts of swinging motion?

It is as well to end our discussion on correct rhythm with a note on how rhythm is associated with power. Imagine yourself on a gear-driven bicycle on a level stretch of road. You put the bicycle into first gear to begin to cycle. You will turn the pedals quickly with your feet but the bicycle itself travels slowly along the road. *The rhythm of your cycling is quick but the bicycle itself is not being powered significantly.* Over a period of time, you will change the gears. The greater the gear chosen, the slower you will pedal the bicycle yet the faster the bicycle itself actually travels. *The rhythm of your cycling is slow but the bicycle itself is being powered significantly.*

Similarly, properly swung short clubs have a quick rhythm but propel the ball insignificant distances. Properly swung longer clubs have slower rhythms but propel the ball significant distances. **Golf sense** is almost like a **nonsense**. It might well explain why **common sense** does not apply. And more "nonsense" is to follow later in this book, this time to help the reader to understand **golf sense**.

ERROR No. 2:   CLUBHEADS FORCED OUT OF THEIR FLIGHT PATHS BEFORE IMPACTING THE BALL:

The core differences between "swinging" action & "hitting" action:
In essence, when one swings the club naturally the clubhead finds its natural flight path itself at the start of the swing. It stays in this natural flight path as it goes around the golfer's stable body until such time as the swing comes to a natural cessation. *It just so happens that the golf ball is struck by the clubhead as it swings around the golfer's stable body.* In other words, some golfers allow the clubhead to impact the ball and rightly so for two reasons.

Firstly, the clubhead should have the appropriate amount of power to move the ball the required *distance*. This amount of power is dictated by the swinging motion of the clubhead as per the relevant length of the shaft. Secondly, the swinging motion of the club should return the clubhead to the position it occupied at address (presumably square) and move the ball *accurately* to its intended target.

The typical naïve golfer, on the other hand, wishes to use the club as a striking implement, to all intents and purposes, with which to hit or beat the ball forward. They do so by *rushing* or *forcing* the clubhead onto the ball with personal force instead of allowing the clubhead to impact the ball through its swinging motion.

But rushing or forcing the clubhead onto the ball with personal force may force the clubhead out of its natural flight path. The naïve golfer is, after all, dictating the flight path the clubhead takes. The naive golfer may not *allow* the clubhead to take its natural flight path because all they want the clubhead to do is to beat or hit the ball forward in their own inimitable way.

This inimitable way, you see, may mean that they dictate the time it takes for the clubhead to impact the ball. But we have already seen how the actions of golfers who swing the clubs are dictated by the time the clubheads take to move in their natural flight paths before they impact the ball. This inimitable way may also mean that the golfer employs the club in such a way that the clubhead may not approach the ball suitably before impact with it. Either way, it is likely that clubhead will not be travelling in its natural flight path just before impact with the ball. It is therefore unlikely to move the ball properly!

Rushing or forcing the clubhead onto the ball with personal force and the possibility of forcing the clubhead out of its natural flight path can be characterised in several ways. Firstly, it should be noted that an abrupt take-away of the club could lessen the chances of the clubhead entering its natural flight path in the first place. If the clubhead fails to enter its natural flight path, it is hardly likely to re-enter it at any stage thereafter before impacting the ball. Secondly, an aggressive swinging of the club following a correct take-away could throw the clubhead out of its natural flight path in its own right. Alternatively, it could de-stabilise the golfer's upper body. And that is even more likely to throw the clubhead out of its natural flight path.

Thirdly, an aggressive swinging of the club on the backswing could move the golfer's head and again destabilise the golfer's upper body with similar repercussions as to its flight path. Fourthly, an aggressive swinging of the club on the downswing could result in bringing the clubhead down sharply onto the ball in order to move it. This action that could have serious repercussions if the loft of that club is low. The following sections of this chapter describe these circumstances.

Finally, it's important to clarify the notion of *"swinging the clubs quickly"*. One golfer can, of course, swing the clubs naturally at a rhythm that is slower or faster than that of another golfer who swings the clubs naturally. We saw in the first chapter, for example, how people have differing physical characteristics. Individual rates of rhythms in themselves do not matter as long as the clubheads remain in their natural flight paths. **Golf sense** is **golf sense** no matter what. And the clubheads invariably remain in their natural flight paths once the golfer intends to swing the clubs naturally and adopts procedures to create same.

The problem, you see, lies with the intention to hit the ball with the clubs with personal force. This can often result in the clubheads of longer clubs, in particular, being forced out of their natural flight paths at some stage before impact with the ball. Why? Because the naive golfer is probably "swinging" the clubs *too quickly!* And they are swinging the clubs too quicky because they are invariably using their energy *excessively* to literally force the clubheads onto the ball to move it.

THE TECHNICAL ANALYSIS OF THE NATURAL GOLF SWING:

When one swings the clubs naturally one does not interfere with the flight paths the clubs take as they go around the golfer's body. The revolution of the swinging motion should generate the power the clubhead requires to move the ball a particular distance and return the clubhead square to the ball to move it to its target.

The golfer thus uses the hands to swing the clubs around the body for swinging sake only. *The golfer's wrists simply rotate in tandem with the hands, arms, shoulders and upper body as they revolve with the clubs around the golfer's person.* In essence, the golfer restrains themself from becoming personally involved in the impacting of the ball and allows the clubhead to do so instead through its swinging motion.

Other golfers, on the other hand, do activate their hand action with the club as the clubhead approaches the ball before impact and during the impact itself. They do so because they wish to increase the momentum of the clubhead so that the impact with the ball will be greater and move the ball further. *Thus, they manipulate the clubheads by activating their wrists to increase the momentum of the clubheads as they are about to impact the*

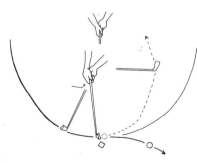

ball. But this increased activity with the wrists/hands has to be very skilled or else the clubhead may not impact the ball squarely.

Other actions with the clubs on the ball may move the ball further distances than the natural swing. But the natural swing is likely to give a greater guarantee of accuracy. If it's accuracy the golfer seeks, they might consider employing some **golf sense** such as the natural golf swing. If it's distance they are after with some *hope* that the ball will fly accurately, they might consider a strategy similiar to using one's **common sense** to hit the ball with the clubs with personal, often indiscriminate, force.

REVISIT THE NATURAL SWING:
Why not revisit the natural swing again and compare it to the "swing" you usually create with the clubs on the golf course. Go to the driving range again. Firstly, recreate the swing as you did in the practise-swinging sessions to date in the driving-range. Repeat the strategies as before in terms of intent (swing the clubs for swinging sake only, grip (primarily with the fingers) and stable central source (keep the body stable throughout). You can close the eyes as before. Alternatively, you could keep them open and employ the spot behind the ball technique again. Just be sure to have someone to observe the flight of the balls for you. Then you can have the confidence to concentrate on making the swing only and not concern yourself with hitting the ball with the clubs with your own force. Nor concern yourself with how far the ball goes.

Now "swing" the clubs to move the ball in your own inimitable way as you do on the golf course. You, assumedly, observe the ball throughout the entire "swing" making process when on the golf course.

Compare the swings. Were the earlier ones with the eyes either closed or focussed on the ground as " forced" as the ones you used as per when you "swing" on the golf course? Was there any significance in the differences of amounts of energy you used to initiate the swinging motion of the longer clubs, in particular? Do you notice any differences between the type of motions the clubs take when they are being taken away at the start of the swing as they are being used? Is one type of motion of the clubs smoother than the other? If so, are there any implications in this?

SECTION 3: THE FIRST CHARACTERISTIC OF EXCESSIVE FORCE: THE ABRUPT TAKE-AWAY:

How the abrupt take-away or "picking the clubhead off the ground" suits the shorter clubs but not the longer clubs:

A golfer who approaches the golf ball with the **common sense** intention to hit it with the club with their own physical force usually wastes no time in doing so. The golfer *"picks"* the clubhead up off the ground abruptly to "wind" the forces of the club up. The golfer then brings the clubhead down onto the ball as quickly as possible. After all, their sole concern is to move the ball with the club with their own, indiscriminate force. So they consequently believe it's best to do so as quickly and as forcibly as possible.

The clubhead takes a steep ascent up by the side of the golfer. As soon as the club reaches the top of the backswing, the golfer's hands brings the club steeply down onto the ball to beat it forward.

Does this flight path brought about by the intention to hit the ball with the clubs with one's own force seem familiar to you? Of course it does – it resembles the less rounded flight paths of naturally swung short clubs. So how successful is this type of action with the shorter clubs?

Well, firstly, the actual contact between clubhead and ball at impact may not be theoretically perfect when the golfer employs "hitting" action with a short club. The angle of descent onto the ball is probably steeper than that pertaining to a naturally swung short club. But the clubface of a short iron is very lofted. So the grooves of the clubface still grip the ball upon impact no matter how steep the angle of impact. The high loft of a short iron gives added "forgiveness", as it were, to a descending blow on the ball regardless of the steepness of its descent.

Thus, the ball still manages to be dragged back along the clubface and the predominant spin imparted onto it should still be backspin. The ball should be forced to rotate from top-to-bottom and not from side-to-side. The ball should be forced reasonably properly forward from the momentum of the overall force. Secondly, the club is still empowered to move the ball the desired distance - short – since very little power has been generated with the steep backswing/downswing of the "hitting" action.

The reality is that if one initiates the swinging motion of a short club incorrectly with an abrupt take-away of the clubhead, the resulting ball flight pattern will not be too adversely affected. The abrupt take-away invariably fails to place the clubhead in its natural flight before impact with the ball. *But the club does not require a lot of swinging motion anyway* since the clubhead moves in a less rounded arc when swung properly. The club does not seem to need **golf sense**.

So if the golfer happened to be using a short club the ball would invariably travel to its intended target. The unsuspecting golfer has no evidence to lead them to believe that their "swinging" action on the ball with short clubs is suspect. So they are likely to persist with what is essentially "hitting" action with the other clubs.

A longer club, on the other hand, *requires a lot of swinging motion* on account of its natural wide and shallow flight path around the golfer's person. This club must enter and remain in its natural flight path for a suitable contact between ball and its *low-lofted clubface* at impact.

Taking the clubhead of a long club off the ground abruptly, however, means that the golfer, not the length of shaft, dictates when the clubhead leaves the ground. The clubhead is not likely to enter its natural wide flight path. Nor is it likely to re-enter it at any stage thereafter. The imparted blow is likely to come down sharply *onto* the ball instead of more down *behind* the ball. The reduced loft of the clubface may not have the same compensatory power as that of a shorter club. The ball is likely to receive a glancing blow that could cause significant amounts of sidespin. This could cause the ball to veer significantly left or right of the target, depending on the type of sidespin. It's now a matter of **Golf Sense Vs. Common**

Sense (or perhaps the more the swinging motion, it more it makes golf sense).

How the situation is made worse:
This confusing situation is often exacerbated with the longer clubs. It makes **common sense** that a golfer requires more energy to initiate the natural swinging motion of a long club than a short club. The strain of the weight of the clubhead on the shaft of a long club is greater than that of a short club as the clubhead lies further away from the golfer with longer clubs. Furthermore, the clubheads of the "woods" (driver, 3 wood, and 5 wood) lie at the end of even longer shafts and are bigger than the clubheads of the long irons. Thus, more energy is required to initiate the natural swinging motion of these longer clubs than the shorter clubs. But the golfer uses only the energy required to initiate the natural swinging motion of any club, be it short or long. It's like the bicycle analogy earlier: it takes more energy to begin to cycle if the bicycle is in a high-speed gear than if it is in a low-speed gear.

But the naïve golfer invariably does not supply this "extra" energy properly. They do not gently push the clubhead of a long club back along the ground with the required amount of energy that is understandably greater than the required amount for a shorter club. *They do so with extra physical force that "picks" the clubhead off the ground unnaturally because they are thinking of the longer distance the ball must travel. This, in their mind according to common sense, requires a more strenuous effort.* Taking long-distance frees in hurling or football, for example, requires greater strength than near-in frees (and let's not forget that the intention to hit the ball with the clubs with one's own force in the first place also encourages the naive golfer to take the club abruptly off the ground). Once again, **common sense** concurs with **golf sense** in theory. But not in practice.

The typical naïve golfer, you see, steps up to the ball and

67

notes how far the ball has to travel. The golfer takes out a long club, for example, a 4 iron, because they "know" this club is suitable for this particular distance. They then look at the ball and say to themselves *"I'd better hit this ball as hard as I can with this club because it has a long way to travel"*. They subsequently whip the clubhead up off the ground as quickly as they can. They then hit or beat the ball as hard as they can with a sharp downward action with the 4 iron, an action we have already noted that is likely to be inappropriate with longer clubs anyway.

As it turns out, once the clubhead has been indiscriminately taken away the damage has probably already been done. The ball will probably fail to travel to its intended target because the clubhead is unlikely to have entered its natural flight path in the first place. And it's only by chance that it might re-enter it before impacting the ball. **Golf Sense Vs. Common Sense.**

Yet when the naïve golfer uses too much force to initiate the "swinging" motion of a short club, the efforts are still reasonably successful. The resultant steep flight path and rhythm are near enough compatible to that of a naturally swung short club!!! The theory espoused at the very beginning of Chapter 1 says that a gentle, smooth take-away of the clubhead of any club is vital to initiate the swinging motion of that club. The reality, however, is that a gentle, smooth take-away of the clubhead of a short club is not vital to initiate the natural swinging motion of that club.

The golfer who uses their **common sense** to pick every clubhead off the ground should return to some **golf sense**. They should bear in mind the first keystone underpinning the natural golf swing - *give the clubs the amount of swinging motion* - whatever the amount - *they require*. At any rate, consistency brings reliability. So the golfer should abide by the theory and maintain a routine of gently and smoothly taking away the clubhead of *every* club to initiate its natural swinging motion - whatever amount of energy it takes to do so. This makes for sound **golf sense**.

So now ask yourself this very important question – when

you play golf at the moment do you take the clubhead away abruptly when initiating the swing? Are you inclined to take a long club away much faster than a short club? Do you see now that you may have been "picking" the clubhead immediately off the ground when initiating the swing? If so, you are now in a position to address this problem.

GOLDEN RULE No. 1:

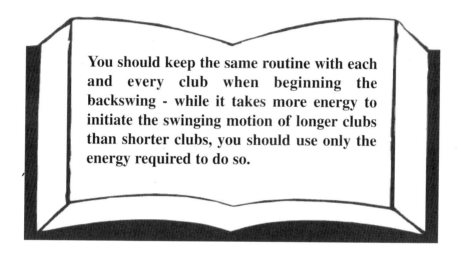

You should keep the same routine with each and every club when beginning the backswing - while it takes more energy to initiate the swinging motion of longer clubs than shorter clubs, you should use only the energy required to do so.

You may have heard the expression *"low and slow"*. Well hopefully now you understand why.

One key, of course, to taking the clubhead away properly is to think of initiating a natural swinging motion with the club rather than thinking of using the club to hit or beat the ball forward with the club with your own strength. Using the appropriate finger grip on the club to sense the strain it takes to initiate the movement of the clubhead along the ground should also encourage the clubhead to enter its natural flight path. And, of course, one can always develop a (golf) sense of how to take the clubhead away appropriately by practise-swinging it a few times.

REVIST THE PRACTISE-SWINGING SESSIONS:

Swing some long clubs with your eyes closed to determine the actual movement of the clubs as they are being swung. Swing the clubs as you normally do on the golf course. Are the motions you create with the longer clubs with your eyes closed smooth, fluid and consistent in their motions? Are your normal swings with these clubs on the golf course more abrupt and/or aggressive? Is a linkage beginning to develop for you between the differing types of motions the clubs take as you employ them as a force/power to move the ball? Is one type of "force" more effective than the other in terms of moving the ball distances *and* accuracy as well? Food for thought?

Correct take-away

Incorrect take-away

70

DISCOVER FOR YOURSELF

Take out a short club and place its clubhead onto the face of a wall or skirting board. Close your eyes and swing. The clubhead should move across the ground and quickly leave the ground without touching the face of the wall or skirting board. Try the same with a longer club. Once again, the clubhead should travel along the ground and take more time to ascend from the ground. Yet the clubhead should not touch the face of the wall/skirting board at any time. Repeat these procedures as you would as if you were on the golf course. Do the clubheads remain untouched by the wall/skirting boards? Is there any difference in the amount of time it takes for either clubhead to ascend from the ground? If not, you can see for yourself that you have been "picking" the clubheads off the ground.

Club against wall

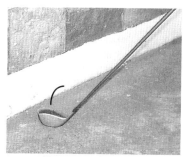

Correct take-away

Incorrect take-away

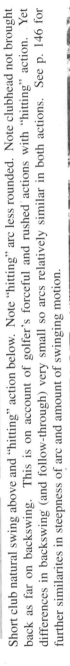

Short club natural swing above and "hitting" action below. Note "hitting" arc less rounded. Note clubhead not brought back as far on backswing. This is on account of golfer's forceful and rushed actions with "hitting" action. Yet differences in backswing (and follow-through) very small so arcs relatively similar in both actions. See p. 146 for further similarities in steepness of arc and amount of swinging motion.

SECTION 4: THE SECOND CHARACTERISTIC OF EXCESSIVE FORCE - THE AGGRESSIVE SWINGING OF THE CLUBS:

PART 1: THE IMPORTANCE OF KEEPING BALANCE/ THE UPPER BODY STABLE DURING THE SWING.

How the aggressive "swinging" of the clubs during the sustenance of the swing often fails to return the clubhead square to the ball at impact:

The intention to hit the ball with the clubs with one's own personal force, you see, can play havoc to the very fabric of natural swinging motion. We have already seen how the naïve golfer could take the clubhead away either abruptly or too forcibly in their determination to literally hit the ball with the club with their own force. The clubhead could fail to enter its natural flight path as a result.

Unfortunately, the naïve golfer could continue the sustenance of the "swing" thereafter aggressively (in the unlikely event that the clubhead ever even entered its natural flight path in the first place). This too aggressive "swinging" of the club inevitably places such strain on the upper body that the stance could be affected and the golfer's central source could become disturbed. *The upper body may not remain stable as the club is being swung.* And one should never forget the importance of a stable upper body in terms of acting as a pivot for the flight path the clubhead takes for the flight path to become natural to the golfer as described in Chapter 1. Thus, the clubhead is unlikely to stay in its natural flight path (if it is there at all) as it is being swung around the golfer's body. So the contact between clubhead and ball at impact is likely to be unsatisfactory.

Once again, this tendency to "swing" the clubs aggressively is understandable. In the first place, this aggressive attitude and rushed action are characteristic to everyday life experiences. In life, for example, we all probably push/pull a door open more abruptly than is necessary. After all, if we were to open it with the minimum amount of force required (gently) we would have to wait a longer amount of time before it is opened. And we would probably feel and look pretty foolish whilst waiting! At times, we are aggrieved with life situations and we literally slam doors such is our frustration! At any rate, the majority of daily chores do not require the attention of the precise force or energy they require on our behalves. Who cares if you open a door abruptly as long as it is opened, for example? Furthermore, the notion of using haphazard or excessive force in our daily lives is reinforced by the fact that many objects are somewhat awkward or heavy. In such circumstances, we have become accustomed to, out of daily habit, to using force aggressively and in a rushed manner. And it cares us not a jot!

Secondly, it's only reasonable to state that an aggressive mental attitude is a hallmark of other ball sports since physical confrontation is predominant in these games. One opponent(s) is in direct competition with another to score the most points through possession and usage of the ball. Thus, for example, the members on one team try valiantly to prevent the other's incursion onto their territory with the ball (for example, tackling in football, hurling, hockey and so on). Or one opponent forces another into making an "unforced error" (for example, by hitting the ball out of bounds in squash or tennis) through aggressive and forceful play.

Furthermore, the tempo or frenzy of the game itself (from its combative nature and the fact that players expend so much energy running around the playing field) surges adrenaline levels. This encourages players to beat the ball forward, very often in a rushed and aggressive fashion. And let's not forget that the ball used in the majority of other ball sports is heavier than the golf ball. Golfers who have experiences of other such sports are consequently used to employing aggression to move the ball in these non-golf games. It's not so much that these actions both on and off the field of play do not make sense. It is, rather, that they become part of a **common sense** that is borne out of experiences and pre-conditioning.

But the typical naïve golfer's aggressive attitude and consequent rushed, hitting action on the ball is the exact opposite to a situation where they could swing the clubs fully, completely naturally and freely without duress. All they have to do is swing the club leisurely in a relaxed manner for maximum results!! After all, there are *no opponents to hamper* the golfer's "swinging" action on the ball with the clubs. The ball remains stationary on the ground before the golfer. It cannot move until such time as the golfer *decides* to impact it with the clubs. This makes **golf sense**. What's the rush for? **Golf Sense Vs. Common Sense.**

DISCERNING SWINGING MOTION AND ITS IMPORTANCE:

How the stance changes with differing clubs:

Take out any short and long club again for your next practise-swinging session. Swing the clubs naturally as before and close you eyes. Concentrate on how your feet respond to the differing degrees of swinging motion associated with the differing clubs. Having taken a *few* swings with each club, you should notice that your stance changes with each club – your feet should have been more apart with the longer club than with the shorter club.

The reason why is again related to the different flight paths the different clubs take when they are swung around the golfer's body. Differing amounts of swinging motion are associated with these flight paths. Your feet should have been most apart with the longer clubs because the body needed maximum stability when the clubheads took the widest flight paths around your body. These wide arcs should have placed significant strain on your body. They should have contained large amounts of swinging motion that was

moving around *and* away from your body. Thus, your mind subconsciously or otherwise should have got you to adjust your feet to accommodate the stress load by widening your stance. If you had placed your feet together, for example, as you swung the driver, you should have lost your balance.

Your body should have tilted and swayed on account of the significant amount of swinging motion being exerted away from your body.

On the other hand, the arcs (or "planes") of the shorter clubs are less shallow. They generate lesser amounts of swinging motion that are less likely to disturb the body. Thus, the feet do not have as much swaying motion to stabilise or support. Once again, your mind subconsciously or otherwise should have got you to adjust your feet accordingly and they should have been much lesser apart than when swinging the longer club.

You swung the clubs several times in the practise-swinging sessions. Your eyes were closed. Your mind was not concentrating on anything else other than making the swinging motions of the differing clubs. In essence, *you took practise-swings with the clubs from which you were able to discern, consciously or otherwise, how*

the different clubs were able to remain in their different yet natural flight paths by adjusting the stance accordingly. One way or another, your feet responded to the amount of swinging motion of each club. They adjusted themselves accordingly to keep the body stable in preparation for the real swing itself.

This brings us back to the core concept of taking some practise-swings with the clubs and discerning the type of motions that accrue so that the natural golf swing in its totality can evolve (Chapter 1). Now that the upper body is stabilised, the golfer has a better chance of ensuring that the clubheads will revolve around their person in their natural flight paths.

The bicycle analogy can help us here again. We have already seen how the bicycle moves faster in a high-speed gear than a low-speed gear although the actual rate of pedalling is slower in the high-speed gear than in the lower-speed gear.

What actually happens is that the cyclist works harder when pedalling the bicycle when it is engaged in the high-speed gear rather than when in the lower-speed gear. Every revolution of the pedal cog turns the high-speed cog more times than the low-speed cog (there are lesser teeth in a high-speed cog than in a lower-speed cog). Thus, the cyclist's body is more likely to sway and move under such duress when cycling in the high-speed gear. The cyclist responds by gripping the handlebars more firmly to stabilise the body. Review the illustration of the cyclists earlier on page 60. Do you notice the grimace on the faster cyclist's face and the stess levels placed on his hands and legs in comparision to the ease on the other cyclist's face, arms and legs?

So, too, does the slower rhythm of naturally swung longer clubs place more physical strain on the golfer's body than does the quicker rhythm of naturally swung shorter clubs. This strain should be catered for by an appropriate stance or else the golfer's body may be destabilised. This may throw the clubheads out of their natural flight paths. The rest you know by now.

We read earlier how a parent could push a child's swing-chair abruptly to begin its swinging motion and how this abrupt action could force the swing out of its natural flight path initially. So too, could a parent push the child's swing-chair too aggressively when sustaining its swinging motion. The child could be thrown off the swing-chair as a result! Similarly, an aggressive swinging of the clubs could destabilise the golfer's body and throw the clubheads out of their natural flight paths.

The "transfer of weight" syndrome:

You may also have noticed another stabilising effect in these practice- swinging sessions. Did you notice how your right leg (of the right-handed golfer) was put under pressure by the backswing of the long clubs? Did you notice as the club came back around your body on the downswing that the pressure eased on the right leg? Did you notice how the left leg then came under pressure from the significant force being exerted away from the body by the swinging motion on the follow-through? Thus, the weight is transferred naturally from one leg to the other in order to keep the body stable and firm throughout the entire swinging process.

This can only happen if one swings these clubs naturally so as to generate the powerful swinging influences in the first place. The feet can then accommodate these de-stabilising influences as a natural consequence. The point is that if one swings a club naturally one is likely to become aware of its swinging motion and influences. Therefore, one is better prepared to cater for these influences. *Hence the importance of practise-swings and discerning the type of motion that accrues from the clubs for further refinement.* And usually one's body parts react to natural swinging motion instinctively if one is not concentrating on anything that distracts one from the swinging motion or its associated influences. This brings us to the second keystone of the natural golf swing - how it influences the golfer in turn.

Some golf teachers think that the golfer should consciously make this "transfer of weight" to create the swing. But the transfer of weight is a consequence of the natural swinging motion because natural swinging motion demands a stable central axis. Otherwise, the clubhead could not stay in its natural flight as it goes around the golfer's body up to the point of impact with the ball. And swinging the club aggressively is very likely to destabilise the golfer's stance that is dependent on the golfer's feet and legs.

DON'T WORRY ABOUT THE DETAIL:

The point above about how the feet respond to the natural swing should *serve as an icon as to how all the components of the natural swing invariably fall into place themselves....*once one participates in the routine of holding the clubs appropriately, closes the eyes or does not focus on the ball and swings the clubs for swinging sake only in practice a few times. The author must explain how the natural golf swing is created and works. But all the reader has to do is to follow the simplistic routine above and everything else - *the golfer's contribution to giving the clubs the amount of swinging motion they require and the golfer's catering for the influences the created swinging motion has on the ball to move it and the golfer* - should fall simply into place without the golfer even thinking consciously about it at times.

HOW THE NAIVE GOLFER OFTEN FAILS TO DISCERN NATURAL SWINGING MOTION:

The naïve golfer simply uses each club to beat the ball forward with their own, indiscriminate strength. These actions are unlikely to generate significant amounts of swinging motion. They are unlikely, then, to discern the influences of natural swinging motions of differing clubs and whether rectifying action, if any, is therefore required.

Secondly, the typical naïve golfer is usually pleased with the outcomes of short clubs when they employ "hitting" action with them. This golfer is likely to employ the longer clubs at least as quickly, if not more quickly, than the short clubs. Their **common-sense** attitude, after all, informs them that the ball should be beaten harder with longer clubs to send it longer distance. *So the golfer's body is likely to become destabilised by such quick "swinging" of these clubs in the first place.*

Other golfers resort to the **golf sense** instead. They simply employ the physical strength or energy required *only* to initiate and sustain the natural swinging motion of the longer clubs. This in itself could generate sufficient influences to de-stabilise the upper body *if the clubs are particularly long.* But the golfer becomes aware of this during a practise-swing and takes a corrective stance to counter-act it. The golfer is further aided in restraining the de-stabilising effects of the swinging motion on the upper body by the fact that the rhythm with which the club is being swung naturally is somewhat slow. After all, the flight paths are wide around the golfer's body. The golfer then simply sustains this swinging motion throughout until it is completed.

The naive golfer, on the other hand, might swing the longer clubs too excessively and take no corrective stance. Even if they did, it may not withstand the de-stabilising effects of the "swinging" motion such could be its excessiveness. Moreover, since the club has probably not been swung naturally, its rhythm is likely to be far quicker than what it should have been. So the chances of de-stabilising the upper body in the first place have probably already increased.

What needs to be understood also is that while the more experienced golfer swings a longer club at a slower rhythm than a shorter one, they do not *consciously* or *purposefully* do so. The rhythm such a golfer uses to swing any club is dictated by the intention to swing the club for swinging sake only. Since the clubs are being swung naturally properly by this golfer it is immaterial to them what the rhythm actually is.

The reality is that the naive golfer rushes both short and long clubs "around" the body since the intention is to hit the ball with the clubs with as much personal force as possible (see photos, p.72 & 100). The more experienced golfer, on the other hand, waits for the clubs to go around the body so that they can impact the ball through their swinging motion instead. The error is not too damaging with shorter clubs. Their natural rhythm is quick. But problems are likely to be encountered with the longer clubs since their natural rhythm is slower than that of the shorter clubs.

This clarification of rhythm dispels another piece of advice often advocated by other golf teachers. How many times have you heard that good golfers swing the driver at the same rate as an eight iron? The advice is well-intentioned since the purpose is for the listener to slow down the rate by which they swing the driver to avoid the flaws described above. But the advice is factually incorrect because a naturally swung driver has a slower rhythm than an eight-iron.

The lesson to be learned is that if your body is de-stabilised on the completion of the swing then you can conclude that you have swung the club too aggressively or with the incorrect rhythm. Your feet, for example, may have moved from the positions they took on the ground before and during the swing. Alternatively, your body may have tilted or swayed excessively and may have been thrown out of canter.

And note how the two keystones underpinning the natural golf swing are inter-connected and converge after some practise-swings. A longer club cannot *receive* the amount of swinging motion it requires if the central source, the golfer's upper body, is destabilised. The clubhead could not then be travelling in its natural flight path. Yet the golfer is made aware of the particular nature of the motion accruing from the club once swung in practise a few times. They can then cater for any *influences* on their body by adopting a corrective stance. This, in turn, gives the club the amount of swinging motion it requires since the clubhead should then be travelling in its natural flight path.

You may have heard the phrase *"it stance to sense."* Interesting one isn't it?

DISCOVER FOR YOURSELF

Why not ask a friend to time your swings with the short club and the long club in the practise-swinging sessions? Your friend should ideally use a stop-watch that emits a "bleep" when the watch is activated. This will help you to correlate the timings of the swing with your friend. You will know if the watch is timing the beginning of the swing and its completion accurately by hearing the respective "bleeps" at these respective points. Get your friend to time the swings you normally make with the clubs on the golf course. The results should be interesting.

AGGRESSION BRINGS THE CLUBHEADS DOWN ONTO THE BALL:

Swinging the clubs aggressively by using one's **common sense**, then, is likely to destabilise the golfer's upper body and throw the clubheads out of their natural flight paths. But let's not forget again that the aggressive attitude of the naive golfer when "swinging" the clubs is also likely to impel them to bring the clubheads sharply down onto the ball to beat it forward. This action, of course, is likely to be incompatible to the low lofts of longer clubs.

Force is all that matters to the golfer who approaches the golf ball with the intention to hit it with the club with their own physical strength. The clubhead is taken up off the ground abruptly and brought back straight down onto the ball as forcefully as possible in order to move it. It's a "double-whammy". The body is likely to become destabilised and the angle of approach likely to be unsuitable. One would wonder what chances the ball could have of being moved properly by a long club in such circumstances? Once again, **common sense,** not **golf sense,** prevails.

REVIST THE NATURAL SWING:

It might be a good idea now for the reader to participate in another practise-swinging session to discern how the feet/legs act to stabilise the upper body. Hopefully, the reader should be able to discern the differing amounts of swinging motion with the differing clubs and adopt corrective stances to cater for same. The reader should hopefully discover how the transfer of weight from one leg to the other comes about from the corrective stance and does not create the swing itself.

While you are there, take some time out to analyse the rhythm by which you swing the different clubs. Do you swing the longer clubs quicker than the shorter ones or vice-versa? Is a connection beginning to develop for you between rhythm and the infamous *power* many naive golfers strive for to move the golf ball? Is your understanding of *power* and how it is created beginning to change for you? Did you create this power to move the ball before on the golf course through abrupt/aggressive actions with the clubs, i.e., through brute force, instead?

Take some time out also to analyse the movement of your head, if any, on the backswing. Pay particular attention to the movement of your shoulders during the swing. Do your shoulders move differently with different clubs? Are the shoulders impeded in any way from moving with the clubs? Are they impeded more by some clubs rather than other ones? Why, do you think?

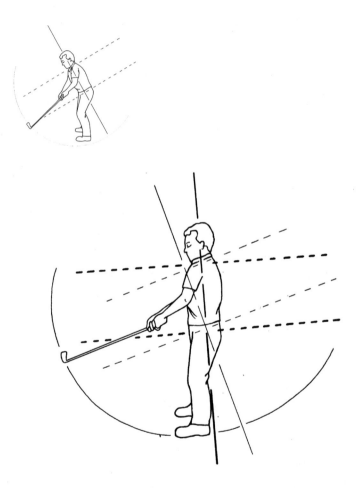

Torso out of natural tilt due to abruptness/aggression with club

SECTION 4: THE SECOND CHARACTERISTIC OF EXCESSIVE FORCE - THE AGGRESSIVE SWINGING OF THE CLUBS (cont.):

PART 2: THE IMPORTANCE OF KEEPING THE HEAD STILL ON THE BACKSWING:

<u>Over-stretching the shoulders, abrupt hinging of the clubs and clearing the chin on the backswing:</u>

Take out a short and long club again and swing them naturally as before. Close your eyes as you swing the different clubs and this time concentrate on the movements your *shoulders* make during the swings. Did you notice how your shoulders followed the flight paths of the clubs? Your shoulders should have moved more or less up and down by your side as you swung the shorter club. The shoulders should have moved more across your body when swinging the longer club. Now pay particular attention to how your left shoulder (if you are a right-handed golfer) behaves on the backswing when using the longer club. As this shoulder approaches your chin, does it collide with it and disturb the head? Or is there clearance such that the shoulder continues to pass under the chin without disturbing the head?

If the golfer adopts a head posture such that it allows the shoulder to pass unhindered by the chin during the backswing, there comes a point when the shoulder eventually stops moving whilst under the chin. The head should remain stable at this point. If the golfer's head does remain stable, the golfer's body itself should also remain stable since a disturbance to the head (from the shoulder colliding with the chin) could disorientate the golfer and cause their body to move.

Some golfers actually stop swinging the longer clubs at this point and begin the downswing. The golfer's head, and consequently, the golfer's body, should remain stationary throughout the change in direction of the clubs. Others continue to "swing" the longer clubs by hinging them upwards from this point until they become horizontal behind the golfer's person. They subsequently bring the clubs down on the downswing. Once again, the golfer's head and body should remain stationary during the change in direction of the clubs since no force has acted upon them to move them, most notably a possible collision between the shoulder and the chin.

Some dangers, however, may arise with the naïve golfer's activities. Firstly, the naïve golfer may continue to swing the longer clubs around the body when the shoulder instead should have stopped at a particular critical point to keep the head stable (assuming no collision took place between shoulder and chin). Secondly, they may hinge the club abruptly.

These actions, of course, are probably associated with the aggressive nature of the more naive golfer. They think they must "swing" more with the longer clubs because the golf ball must travel longer distances. But if the head is tilted by an over-exaggeration of the shoulders on the backswing the golfer may become disorientated. The body may be moved as a result and the clubhead may be thrown out of its natural flight path during the backswing. And it will be very difficult, if not impossible, for it to re-enter it again when it matters most – just before impact with the ball on the downswing.

And let's not forget that clearing the chin in the first place is vital to creating the natural swing properly. As the shoulder approaches the chin on the backswing, it should not collide with it or it may disturb or tilt the head. This may dis-orientate the golfer and the golfer's balance may be disturbed. Thus, some golfers adopt a head posture such that it allows the shoulder to pass unhindered by the chin during the backswing. This factor is described in more detail in Chapter 4.

These are further warning mechanisms for noting your possible too aggressive swinging of the clubs. Once again, these are actions that are unlikely to affect the shorter clubs significantly since short clubs do not go around the body as such. But the longer clubs do go around the golfer's body and are liable to cause such difficulties. These, then, are further components that need to be factored in correctly through practise-swings.

It should be noted that it is often difficult to keep the head completely still on the backswing. When this happens, what matters is that the head rotates in tandem with the motion of the backswing as this should not harm the creation of the motion itself. The head, in effect, turns parallel to the swinging motion and does not affect it. If the head tilts, however, it is likely to affect the quality of the swinging motion of the club on the backswing since the tilt may affect the golfer's balance as the club is being swung. Indeed, some golfers consciously rotate the head to trigger a smooth take-away with the club since they find this action facilitates a smooth rotation of the torso itself.

DISCOVER FOR YOURSELF

Put yourself on a plank of wood supported by two crates. Swing a short club. No matter how you swing this club or what way you position your stance you will invariably stay on the plank. Now swing a longer club. If you swing this club haphazardly or aggressively or if your chin collides with your shoulders or if your stance is too narrow you should soon understand the importance of a stabilising stance and correct rhythm!

<u>The difference between aggressive swinging & aggressive golfing</u>:

While a case can often be made to play golf aggressively, that is, attempting to propel the golf ball as near as possible to the pin, one should be cautious of swinging the clubs themselves aggressively. The typical naive golfer invariably employs the longer clubs in this way because it makes **common sense** to do so. After all, the ball needs to be moved long distances. Previous experience in other ball sports on behalf of the naive golfer, if any, also support this reasoning since the harder the ball is hit in these sports, the further it travels. These actions, however, invariably bring about inconsistent results in terms of moving the ball accurately to its target since the clubs are invariably thrown out of their natural flight paths as a result. Indeed, the reader may recall the competitive nature of the aggressive actions of the "swing-ball" players earlier that result in the ball moving in unpredictable flight paths.

When swinging a club, one could be well advised to swing it without putting undue duress on the upper body or head. The flight paths of the clubheads are unlikely to be consistent to the golfer if the upper body sways or if the head tilts as the clubs are being swung. One should therefore try to avoid using abrupt and/or aggressive energy when swinging the clubs. **Golf sense** suggests a different method - *try to swing within oneself, to swing the clubs within one's physical capabilities.*

While we often look to professional golfers as role models in how to swing the clubs properly, there can be dangers in watching them as they actually swing the clubs. Swinging the clubs within one's physical capabilities is a case in point. Some professional golfers swing somewhat quickly. Others swing somewhat more slowly. But each professional golfer swings to their physical instincts and capabilities. They respect, not flout, the characteristics of swinging motion regardless of their particular rhythm. A naive observer might think, however, that the clubs should be swung as quickly as possible because they saw a particular professional golfer swing that way. But a quick tempo may not, and usually is not, suited to the reflexes of a golfer who plays the game occasionally.

So now ask yourself a second very important question – when you play golf at the moment do you "swing" the clubs aggressively? Can you discern the tell-tale signs of swaying upper body, loss of balance and tilting of the head on the backswing? Do you force the clubhead sharply down onto the ball with aggression? If so, you are now in a position to address this problem.

89

GOLDEN RULE No. 2:

The golfer should keep the same routine with each and every club when sustaining its swinging motion - use only the energy required to sustain the swinging motion of each club, be it long or short, and consequently swing the club with the correct rhythm. To help the golfer to do so, they should swing each and every club within the physical capabilities of their body.

The final word on aggressive swinging is again linked to the bicycle analogy. You can never cycle a bicycle too quickly because the chain is the physical link between you (your feet on the pedals) and the back wheel. The faster you pedal, the faster the bicycle will travel until you cannot travel any faster (eventually, of course, the chain will break over a period of time when you will have placed too much strain upon it). On the other hand, there is no physical link between you as you hold the clubs and the golf ball. No physical element can prevent you from swinging the clubs too quickly. But a psychological element may - if you consciously think about swinging the clubs for swinging sake only.

SECTION 5: HOW PRACTISE-SWINGS BECOME THE SAFETY NET:

The point has already being made that a practise-swing or two fore-warns the golfer of any possible influences that might affect the creation of natural swinging motion with the clubs. The golfer then caters for these influences by making necessary adjustments. These practise-swings act as a checklist or safety check to ensure that natural swinging motion can be created properly by the golfer.

Moreover, there is no absolute guarantee that when a club enters its natural flight path at the beginning of the swing that it will stay there on the continuation of that swing. Furthermore, while the natural golf swing can be employed constantly with any club, the natural swing amongst the clubs themselves is not constant since these characteristics change as the length of the club shaft changes. In these instances, then, practise-swings act more than simple safety checks - they become a necessity. Let's look at these practise-swings in more detail.

THE THEORY OF PRACTISE-SWINGS:

The reader is by now familiar with the correct procedure regarding the take-away of the clubs. But while the clubhead may be in its natural flight path, it may be swinging quite freely on account of the facilitating (finger) grip. The clubhead may not necessarily stay in its natural flight path as it is being swung "around" the golfer's body if the golfer's stance cannot stabilise the upper-body against the swinging motion. This is particularly the case if it is a significant amount of swinging motion accruing from a long club.

The golfer can take a practise-swing with the club and react accordingly to the free-flowing movement of the clubhead as it influences the upper-body by adopting a corrective stance. The hitherto free-flowing and possibly de-stabilising swinging motion of the clubhead should now take a definite shape in its swinging motion on account of the golfer's adjusted stance and consequent stable upper-body. The flight paths the club takes should now be genuinely natural to the golfer since the upper-body is acting as a pivot "around" which the clubheads now revolve.

The golfer's head posture should be such that the head is not moved on the backswing. This could occur if the shoulders collide with the chin or if the golfer over-swings or hinges the clubs too abruptly on the backswing. In either case, the clubheads could be thrown out of their natural flight paths. Once again, a practise-swing should inform the golfer if the head is being moved by whatever means and the golfer can make adjustments if so required.

When these components are factored in, the energy to swing the club in this now consistent, defined flight path that is natural to the golfer becomes consistent in itself. *The club is travelling in a defined flight path that has a defined amount of swinging motion associated with it through the practise-swings already.* By now, the golfer should have been informed of how much energy is required only to move (swing) the clubhead in this flight path. Thus, the clubhead should hopefully be swung at its correct rhythm when impacting the ball for real.

And since the golfer takes a practise-swing or two in total with any club (two practise-swings should inform the golfer of all the necessary requirements and adjustments), the golfer becomes aware of the precise idiosyncratic nature of the characteristics of the natural swinging motion of that club.

It's either a friendly or vicious circle. If all of the components are factored in correctly, the natural golf swing should evolve. If one component is not factored in correctly, it can seriously affect the quality of the natural swing. Not that it matters that much to the short clubs since they do not require swinging motion in effect.

It may be prudent, then, for the amateur golfer to take practise-swings with the clubs immediately before making the swing for real on the golf course itself. The golfer should concentrate on the arbitrary type of swinging motion being created initially and analyse how it can be shaped properly into natural swinging motion.

This concentration can be aided by either closing the eyes or by focussing on a spot of ground as the clubs are being swung in practise. This should enable the golfer to swing the clubs very near to, if not the correct, natural swinging motions of these clubs. In such circumstances, the golfer is unlikely to use any excessive energy when employing the clubs since no incentives exist to do so.

PRACTISE-SWINGS IN ACTION:

Thus, for example, one might be using a three-iron. A practise swing with the club should educate the golfer on what corrective stance to adopt, if any. The golfer may perceive, for example, that the previous club used, for example, a wedge, had lesser swinging motion so that stance should have been quite narrow.

But the three-iron should be accompanied with a more significant amount of swinging motion so the stance may have to be adjusted and made broader. The stance should not be vastly broader as long as the clubs are not being swung aggressively. The golfer then checks if the head is being moved on the backswing by taking another practise-swing with the three-iron. The head posture may not have been particularly important with the wedge since there is little swinging motion associated with this club. As for shoulder/chin collision, for example, the shoulders should not have been coming around the golfer's body as such on the backswing with that particular club. Furthermore, the completion of the backswing is reached before the chin could collide with the shoulders anyway. As for over-swinging and abrupt hinging with the wedge, there was hardly any swinging motion with it in the first place!

But the three-iron has more swinging motion associated with it than the wedge. The shoulders should indeed come around the golfer's body and are more likely to collide with the chin unless the head posture is adjusted to prevent any possible collision. The golfer may very well over-swing or hinge the club abruptly because the club was being swung in the first place. *But these latter two factors can also be overcome if the golfer observes some **golf sense** and adopts the rule of swinging the clubs within their physical capabilities (which is more likely if the eyes are being employed correctly and the club taken away properly at the beginning).* So if the golfer does indeed swing the three-iron within their physical abilities during the practise-swings, the only tangible factor to be monitored is whether the shoulders collide with the chin to disturb the head.

Now that these components are factored in, the energy to swing the club should become consistent to its now defined flight path that is natural to the golfer. By now the golfer should have been fore-warned, as it were, that the rhythm should be slower and the energy required to swing the three-iron would be greater than that of the wedge. So the golfer should accept these changes as the club is being swung. Thus, the clubhead of the three-iron should be swung at *its* correct rhythm when impacting the ball for real.

It all revolves around respecting the amount of swinging motion exhibited by a club, does n't it? (if you pardon the pun).

THE REALITY OF THE PRACTISE-SWINGS

The golfer who intends to hit the ball with a club with personal force takes a practise-swing usually to prepare themselves on *how hard* to hit the ball with that club with personal force. On the other hand, the golfer who intends to swing a club for swinging sake only takes a practise-swing or two with that club to educate themselves on the nuances of the (swinging) motion of that club. This helps them replicate these nuances for real when swinging the club to move the ball. The practise-swings thus give the golfer adequate preparations, both mental and physical, to create the swing naturally for real to move the ball.

Sometimes, the most likely factor to account for during the practise-swings is not related to the physical quality of the (swinging) *motions* of the clubs themselves but rather to the physical positioning of the golfer's head during the actual swing. Every golfer has to look down to see the ball before they attempt to move it. But the typical naive golfer who looks *down* to see the ball may not be aware that this posture can physically interfere with the motions of the clubs as they are taken on the backswing. They may never check to determine whether or not their downward gaze is such that the shoulder could collide with the chin and disturb the (swinging) motions of the clubs.

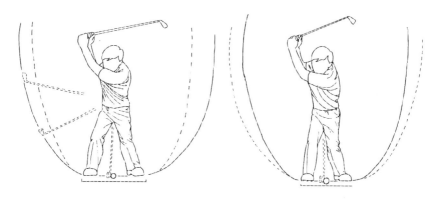

3-iron swing characteristics (full line) Wedge characteristics (dotted line)

Wedge swing characteristics (full line). 3-iron characteristics (dotted line).

Taking practise-swings and corrective adjustments are easy. The natural golf swing is very easy to create in practise. The problem is in replicating it for real on the golf course. What's the difference? Could it have anything to do with the fact that no ball and target exists when taking a practise-swing? Food for thought yet again?

THE BOXER ANALOGY:

In many ways, a naive golfer is like a naive boxer in terms of how they employ their physical strength as a force.

A naïve boxer may, for example, deliberately concentrate on pounding the other boxer's torso with blows successively. The more experienced boxer may save his strength and weave in and out of confrontation with the other boxer. He may simply bide his time to concentrate his blows to the other boxer's chin. All he needs is one proper, *square* connection to the chin and the bout is won. And since the naive boxer expends more energy overall during the bout it is more likely that this boxer will leave his chin more unguarded as the contest continues.

So too, does the more experienced golfer employ a lesser amount of strength than the typical naive golfer. The more experienced golfer uses a lesser amount of energy to swing the clubs only. They move the ball through the swinging motion of the clubs. This gives a greater guarantee of square contact between

ball and clubface at impact. The naïve golfer uses more energy than the more experienced golfer. But this excessive energy is often mis-

placed because the chances are less likely that the clubhead will make *square* contact with the ball upon impact.

REVIST THE SWING:

Once again, the reader is advised to return to some practise-swing sessions. The participant should try to analyse the various components of the natural swing as they have evolved in this chapter. Check for correct take-away, correct head posture, correct stance and correct rhythm with various clubs.

Correct rhythm is vital. Visit the driving range to determine if the rhythm of your swinging action on the ball with the differing clubs is indeed correct. Do not be surprised if you find that it is easier to create the correct rhythm in the practise-swinging sessions since your eyes are closed and no ball exists. Notwithstanding this, use the spot of ground behind the ball technique on the driving range and try again to determine differences, if any, between the swinging motions of long clubs and shorter ones. The difficulty, of course, lies in keeping your eyes on the spot of ground as the clubhead impacts the ball and as the ball leaves the clubface.

Once again, ask a friend to monitor the flight of the ball as soon as it leaves the clubface. Now you can concentrate on that spot of ground behind the ball and not worry about the ball. Your friend will inform you of where it has flown to and how far it has travelled. Do the results surprise you? Does this technique seem as absurd now as you may have thought earlier?

RECAPITULATION:

(i) "Hitting" action can be best defined as the naïve golfer's intention to literally hit the ball with the clubhead with their own force just as a tennis player, for example, hits the tennis ball with the racket with their own force. When employing this action, the naïve golfer brings the clubhead up sharply off the ground and then down sharply onto the ball as forcibly as possible. Any golfer, of course, must hit the ball with the clubhead in order to move it. It simply makes **common sense** to propel the golf ball in this way.

(ii) But certain errors can arise from this "hitting" action and these errors are most noticeable when the naïve golfer uses the longer clubs. The naive golfer thinks that one should hit the ball as hard as one can when using the longer clubs because they think this excessive, indiscriminate force is required to move the ball long distances. This means that they employ such clubs aggressively.

Firstly, hitting the ball as hard as one can when using the longer clubs could result in not giving the clubhead the time it requires to return square to the ball at impact. Secondly, their aggressive "swinging" of the club with personal force is likely to force the clubhead out of its natural flight path through a destabilisation of the golfer's body. Furthermore, their aggressive "swinging" of the club often results in their bringing the clubheads down steeply onto the ball. In any instance it may be possible that the naïve golfer has generated sufficient force to move the ball the desired long distance. But the actual contact between ball and clubhead at impact will most likely be inappropriate and the ball will probably veer away from its intended target.

(iii) But shorter clubs require little amounts of swinging motion so "hitting" action can suffice. Unfortunately, the naïve golfer may not be aware of this and can become confused. However, since using one's **common sense** in employing "hitting" action with the short clubs brings reasonable success, they usually persevere with this strategy with the longer clubs with resulting uncertain success.

(iv) The intention to hit the ball with the clubs with one's own force can also be suspect when initiating the swinging motions of the clubs. This intention brings with it an abrupt take-away of the clubhead off the ground. The golfer themself takes the clubhead off the ground. This action is not very damaging with shorter clubs since they leave the ground quite quickly naturally at the beginning of their swinging motion. But this action can be quite damaging to longer clubs since they spend more time travelling along the ground before entering their natural flight paths than do the shorter clubs.

(v) The naïve golfer's way of thinking may need analysis. Using one's **common sense** to move the ball by hitting it with one's own, often indiscriminate, physical strength can lead to the use of an excessive method of employment of force. This can bring inconsistent outcomes when moving the ball to its target. Using **golf sense** to concentrate on swinging the clubs alone may lead to the use of a more correct employment of force. This can generate an appropriate force to move the ball and it can also give a greater likelihood of the clubhead impacting the ball squarely to send it to its intended target. **Golf Sense Vs. Common Sense.**

Thus far we have seen how the golfer caters for the influences of the swinging motion by adjusting the stance and allowing the clubhead to impact the ball through its swinging motion. There remains one other factor to be catered for yet. Chapter 3 deals with this.

Long club "natural" sequence above, "hitting" sequence below. Note width of arc of "natural" compared to "hitting". Note backswing of "hitting" shorter than that of "natural" and how follow-through of "natural" is not as completed as that of "natural". These denote the golfer's rush to employ the club to hit the ball and the golfer's anxiety to observe the ball with "hitting" action. Note the smoothness of the motion of the natural club whereas the motion of the "hitting" is more abrupt and broken. See p.146 for disparity in steepness and amount of swinging motion between "natural" & "hitting".

CHAPTER 3: HOW COMMON-SENSE OFTEN SEES AND DECEIVES:

SECTION 1: THE DANGERS OF OBSERVING THE BALL BEFORE AND AFTER IMPACT:

BEFORE IMPACT:

It makes **common sense** that if one wishes to hit the ball with the clubhead one should focus on it so that one can hit it. After all, we watch things as we hit them in every day life experiences. However, while it seems normal that one must focus on an object to hit it, so too, it seems, can the very observation of an object reinforce our sub-conscience to hit the object as hard as possible.

Watching something with a striking implement in hand seems like a self-fulfilling prophecy to literally hit that something. Self-fulfilling prophecies take their origin from the mythological King Pygmalion of Cyprus. He fell in love with an ivory statue of a woman and asked Aphrodite, the Goddess of Love, to send him a woman like the statue. Aphrodite put life into the statue instead. This "Pygmalion Effect" is evident in many real life situations today. In educational psychology, for example, research has shown that students whose teachers have high expectations of them perform better academically than students whose teachers have lesser expectations of them.

Observing the ball before and during the swing, then, *could be* a very dangerous activity. The first trap the gullible golfer may fall into is when they have addressed the ball and are ready to initiate the "swing." The golfer may have the intention to swing the club naturally and allow the ball to be moved through the swinging motion of the club. But the very fact that the gullible golfer focuses on the ball as they take away the clubhead may *trigger* thoughts of having to use their own force to hit the ball with the club as hard as they can. Thus, they might "pick" the clubhead off the ground abruptly and the clubhead might never enter its natural flight path.

The situation may also become quite hazardous if the naive golfer watches the ball during the swing itself. If, for some bizarre reason, the clubhead manages to stay in its natural flight path from the (abrupt) take-away, it could be quickly thrown out of this path as the golfer continues the swing. Once again, the observation of the ball could trigger thoughts of hitting the ball with the club as hard as possible with subsequent aggressiveness. After all, the naive golfer sees the ball in front of them. As far as they are concerned, this needs to be *hit* by them.

In either case, one's observation of the ball before or during the swing may change the initial intention of swinging the clubs naturally into an intention to hitting the ball with the clubs with one's own strength. Or it may transform one's intention to hit the ball with the clubs with one's own force into a determination to hit the ball as hard as one can with one's own force. In either case, the observation of the ball before and during the swinging process could mean that the naive golfer might think of nothing other than hitting the ball with the club with personal force. The thought of swinging the club naturally - **golf sense** - might leave or never even enter their head. The result, of course, is the infamous "hitting" action on the ball that is abrupt, aggressive and downward onto the ball. And this is fine with shorter clubs but what about the longer ones?

Naïve golfers who have had or who continue to enjoy other ball sports are even more prone to suffer this type of self-fulfilling prophecy. Players in other ball sports are constantly watching the ball because they have to. They must concentrate on the ball as it traverses the field of play since possession of the ball is everything. If you don't have the ball you cannot score. Furthermore, the physical pressure applied by an opponent further intensifies a player's focus on the ball. The player is only too well aware that the opposing player could interfere with or impede the ball just before the moment of striking impact. *The fact remains that one should be very disciplined when observing the ball before impact between ball and clubhead not to fall into this trap.*

REVISIT THE NATURAL SWING:

Go to the driving-range. Adopt the routine you usually adopt on the golf course. Keep your eyes on the ball at all times during the swing-making process. Are you confident that you can observe the ball and restrain yourself from hitting the ball with the clubs with your own force? If so, congratulations!

If you have doubts, however, why not try the the spot of ground behind the ball technique again. Does this help you create the swing naturally since no ball now exists for you to hit with the clubs? Once again, ask a friend to monitor the flight of the ball as soon as it leaves the clubface. This should give you greater confidence to restrain yourself from observing the ball itself. Are you beginning to wonder if the real skill in moving the ball is psychological rather than physical?

AFTER IMPACT:

It seems very obvious that one observes an object to see where it has gone once one has hit it in order to move it. This is particularly the case if one had in mind a desired destination for the object. So one is surely going to use one's **common sense** to see if it reached that location or not once it has been hit.

This desire to see if the ball has reached its intended destination or not once moved by a player is very common in non-golf ball sports. The ball is used to score points by sending it to a specific target, for example, through the basket in basketball or through the scoring posts in football. Players in these games are naturally anxious to see if they have scored points with the ball so they look up to observe the flight of the ball as soon as they have struck it. Players require possession of the ball in order to contribute to a scoring movement or to keep the ball away from the opposition. Players, then, are anxious to see if they have passed the ball properly onto fellow players as these actions will hopefully lead to a score or keep the opponents at bay. Indeed, everybody – players/opponents and spectators alike - looks at the ball at all times because everything depends on the ball and where it is going as it continually traverses the field of play.

If anything, golfers should be even keener to observe the flight path of the golf ball than players in other ball sports for a variety of reasons. Players in non-golf sports, for example, are never concerned about losing the ball because the playing area is relatively small in comparison to the wide boundaries of a golf course. In addition, the golf ball often travels far greater distances than the ball in other sports. Even if the ball is lost in non-golf sports, a replacement ball is quickly thrown in so the game can continue without penalisation to either team.

But if a golfer loses a ball they are penalised. And losing strokes severely dents a golfer's chances of winning in competition since the golfer with the least amount of strokes wins. There are very few, if any, visual impediments to locating the ball in other ball sports whereas in golf the ball can end up in extreme rough or amidst trees or bushes.

Moreover, golfers are often confronted by hazards such as bunkers on the fairway or water surrounding the greens. The naïve golfer who is unsure of their game at the best of times would have even greater anxiety to see where the ball goes after impact with the club when confronted by such hazards.

Most important of all, golf is very often an individual game with one player in direct competition against others. The golf ball is *your* golf ball. Others may not be too concerned about where your ball is going nor overly concerned about looking for it if it has flown out of sight. All of these circumstances combined can conspire to impel the typical naïve golfer to look up to see where the golf ball is going as soon as it is struck by the clubhead. And, to be fair, understandably so as well.

<u>Why it can be unwise to observe the flight of the golf ball as soon as it has been impacted by the clubhead:</u>

However, if a golfer looks up to see where the golf ball is going as soon as it is struck by the clubhead there is a very good chance that they will forget about utilising the club to complete the swinging motion of the club. *And the natural golf swing cannot be created properly unless it is completed properly.* This is **golf sense**. The golfer who typically fits this bill is, of course, the one who intends to hit the ball with the clubs with their own force. After all, the intention is to hit the ball. The ball is their sole concern. Once the ball has been "hit" by the clubhead, this golfer is going to use their **common sense** to instinctively look up to see where the golf ball is going. The club is forgotten about in the process and the swing is never completed. We will see soon how other golfers, on the other hand, focus on making the natural swing with the clubs and how they respect its characteristics to observe the flight of the ball. **Golf Sense Vs. Common Sense.**

<u>Why complete the swing if the ball has been impacted by the clubhead anyway?</u>

One might well argue that there is no need to complete the swinging motion of the club once the clubhead has impacted with the ball. Well, it may well be possible that the clubhead impacts with the ball and the golfer can look up immediately to follow the flight path the ball takes after impact. But that does not necessarily mean that the clubhead has gone through the ball properly at impact. And this could happen if the golfer looks up quickly to observe the flight path of the ball as soon as it leaves the clubface.

Furthermore, the reader should remember the sole purpose of this book. It is to get the typical naïve golfer to understand that the natural swing is probably a more reliable method of moving the ball than hitting it with the clubs with one's own, often indiscriminate, force. And natural swinging motion has a natural beginning, a natural middle and a natural end. The golfer cannot

105

create swinging motion naturally unless they initiate the swinging motion, sustain it and complete it. If you want to cook your dinner properly you must leave it in the oven for the required amount of time. You cannot take it out of the oven halfway through and expect it to be wholesome and eat it, can you?

LESSON NO. 10:

> The completion of the natural swing is part and parcel of the dynamic of the natural swing itself. The completion of the natural swing is an instrinsic characteristic of the natural swinging motion itself so the natural golf swing can never be created properly unless it is completed properly.

But surely a golfer has to look up to see where the golf ball is going? How else can the ball be located? And the reality is that some golfers do indeed look up to see where the golf ball is going...but not as soon as it leaves the clubface after impact. They look up to see where the golf ball is going at a more appropriate time.

SECTION 2: HOW NATURAL SWINGING MOTION MOVES THE GOLFER'S HEAD:

How the golfer reacts to the swinging motions of the clubs:

The swinging motion of a club around a golfer's body generates an amount of power onto its clubhead that moves the ball upon impact with it. It also generates an equal amount of power that can influence the golfer's body/torso in turn. However, it does not influence the golfer's body/torso as profoundly as the golf ball. The mass of the golfer's body/torso is significantly greater than that of the golf ball so the body presents greater resistance to being moved by the swinging motion. Notwithstanding this, the influences created by swinging the longer clubs around the golfer's body is significant such that the golfer may have to open the stance to its fullest in order to cater for possible destabilising effects.

But the golfer's torso is not the only body part that is influenced by the swinging motions of the clubs. The golfer's head is influenced even more than the torso because it is of less mass than the torso itself. It is thus more prone to the influences of the swinging motions of the clubs. And, not surprisingly, the longer the club, the more the head is influenced by the swinging motion accruing from that club. So the golfer should cater for these influences as well.

How the swinging motion of a club influences the moving of the golfer's head

The reader should now participate in another practice-swinging session to discern how the swinging motions of a short and long club move the golfer's head.

Did you notice for yourself how your head was moved to some slight extent by the insignificant swinging motion of the short club whereas the swinging of the longer club moved your head significantly more? Your head should hardly have been altered when you brought the short club back on the backswing since the clubhead went up by your side and not around your back as such. Your head should also not have been moved significantly on the downswing itself but should have been influenced somewhat more on the follow-through. Its momentum was greater and your head would have been moved upward to some extent with the steep follow-through of the club in its latter stages.

The backswing of the longer club should have moved your head to a greater extent since your shoulders were coming across your body (yet under your chin, note correct head posture, Chapters 2 & 4). If, however, you had been concentrating on the ball, the backswing of the longer club may have put sufficient stress on your head to move it (hopefully not to tilt it). But not enough to move the focus your eyes had on the ball.

However, the swinging motion of the longer club on the follow-through should have moved your head significantly whether you wanted your head to remain stable or not. This is actually quite difficult to determine if your focus is on the ball as you swing the clubs. You can carry out two tests to verify that the swing does indeed move the head significantly when using the longer clubs.

Firstly, you could take out a long club, a driver, for example, and concentrate on a spot of ground behind an imaginary golf ball. Hopefully, your eyes should remain focussed on this spot of ground during the backswing despite the stress such a swinging motion should place on your head. Your focus on the spot of ground should remain firm on the downswing. The momentum of the follow-through should be much greater, however, than that of the downswing. It should move your head horizontally. Your eyes should be focussing on a spot of ground some inches ahead of the original spot of ground by the time the swing has been completed. Alternatively, you could simply close your eyes as you swing the (long) club from beginning to completion and note how your head is moved on the follow-through stage of the swing.

This puts a particular complexion on the much-advocated advice to *"keep the head still"* during the swing. We have already seen how important it is for the golfer to keep the head still on the backswing (often not completely still) but the notion of keeping the head still thereafter requires clarification.

Some golfers can employ body parts such as the feet to resist the swaying influence the swinging motion can have on the torso both on the backswing, downswing and follow-through. One can, of course, use one's neck muscles to resist the influence of the swinging motion to move one's head on the follow-through with the longer clubs (see below). But such action is unnecessary since it is *natural* for the natural swinging motion of a golf club to move the golfer's head.

When the head is actually moved by the swinging motions of the clubs and how such movement is a characteristic of the natural swinging motions of the clubs:

The movement of the head, then, is a natural *consequence* of the swinging motion of the clubs, that is, the swinging motion of the clubs themselves move the golfer's head, not the golfer. But the golfer's head is moved not simply during the swing itself but during the follow-through stage. Since these influences on the golfer occur naturally from the swinging motion of the club, the golfer should allow these influences to take place in order for natural swinging motion to take its course and effect. This is the very nature of natural swinging motion and it has to be respected by all – beginner golfers, high-handicap golfers, good golfers and professional golfers. Note that the head is moved significantly more with the longer clubs than the shorter ones on the follow-through.

Alternatively, of course, the golfer could enforce some restraint on the head through exercising the neck muscles. They could then move the head personally at some time late in the follow-through. Many golfers play golf so regularly that these muscles become acclimatised to such strain and their neck muscles literally bulge under such duress. And this phenomenon is apparent in other sports as well. Grand prix racing drivers, for example, endure tremendous stress levels on their necks on account of the G-forces they experience as they speed so quickly in their cars. Their regimented practise routines condition the neck muscles to this pressure.

But the amateur golfer should let the swinging motion move their head when it should naturally do so. Their neck muscles may not be so well conditioned to such personal enforcement as those who play golf very regularly. Enforcing restraint on the neck can be physically discomforting if not damaging to both the neck and lower spine/back. Remember: the bottom-line is that a*ll that matters is that the golfer does not observe the flight of the ball prematurely.*

How the premature moving of the head to observe the ball with a short club is less damaging than when using a long club:
The practice of moving the head up abruptly to observe the flight path of the ball as soon as it leaves the clubface is not too damaging with the shorter clubs. First, it should be noted that the head is *not greatly influenced* by the follow-through of the swinging motion itself in general since little swinging motion is being generated in the first place. The head remains stable until well into the follow-through stage. But the natural rhythm of the short clubs is quite *quick* and the head is moved *upward* by the steep follow-through of these clubs.

In reality, the naïve golfer's instinctive *quick* looking *up* to see where the ball is going immediately after impact with the clubhead is not too far removed from what should have been the result of the influence of the swinging motion on the golfer anyway. The core issues are that the follow-through of a naturally swung short club is steep and short and the ball is moved short distances with these clubs. Prematurely observing the ball does not affect the steepness or length of the follow-through too adversely. Nor does it affect the distance the ball travels since the distance is quite short anyway. Thus, this **common sense** reaction is not very damaging to the "swing" in such circumstances.

The real danger, however, is that the naïve golfer might think that the quick, upward movement of the head to observe the ball as soon as it leaves the clubface is also acceptable when using the longer clubs. This, in fact, is contrary to what the natural reaction of the golfer's head should have been as dictated by the swinging motion of longer clubs.

The rhythm of the longer club is slower than that of a naturally swung short club. It would take a longer time for the follow-through to begin to influence the moving of the head. Yet the naïve golfer moves the head to observe the flight path of the ball once it has left the clubface just after immediate contact between the ball and the clubhead. This contact/impact occurs just at the very beginning of the follow-through when its influence would be at its *weakest* and would hardly move the head at all.

Furthermore, when the follow-through motion would move the head, it would be moved *significantly*. The amount of power as generated by the swinging motion of the longer club would be quite large. But the golfer's quick looking up to observe the flight of the ball would not allow such significant movement to take place. And to put the final nail in the coffin, the direction in which the head would be moved significantly would be *horizontal* not vertical. And naive golfers look *up* to see the ball's flight as soon as the ball has left the clubface.

Basically, the swinging motion of the clubhead of a long club should move the golfer's head some time after the ball has been impacted with the clubhead. This occurs at some point late in the follow-through stage when its influence is greatest. It should not move the golfer's head as soon as the impact happens at the very beginning of the follow-through stage. This occurs when its influence is barely noticeable. Thus, the golfer who looks up as soon as the ball is impacted is not allowing natural swinging motion to take its course. They cannot expect to benefit fully from its propelling nature. *The golf club is neglected and the follow-through is shortened considerably as the swinging motion is not completed fully.* **Golf Sense Vs. Common Sense.**

Once again, it's becoming evident that it's all about the amount of swinging motion a club exhibits when swung naturally and respecting it!

REVISIT THE NATURAL SWING:

Go to the driving-range. Check to see if you do, indeed, observe the flight of the ball prematurely. You may recall that you have been advised already to ask a friend to observe the ball's flight for you in previous practise-swinging sessions. Now try it for yourself.

Start with the shorter clubs. These clubs exert little swinging motion to influence the moving of your head. But the shoulders come up quickly on the follow-through. It's pointless, almost, to try to restrain yourself from moving your head when the club is well on in its follow-through.

Graduate to the middle irons. These clubs exert significant amounts of swinging motion after the follow-through stage. These will test your mental resolve although the effects of the swinging motion come early enough on the follow-through.

The real test is with the long clubs. These exert very significant swinging motions on your head *late* on the follow-through. Furthermore, they move the ball the longest distances so your anxiety to observe the ball might be at its greatest. Take time out to practise-swing these clubs with your eyes closed to re-assure yourself when and how the swinging motion moves your head. Practise, practise and practise again.

The single most important point to note regarding premature observation of the ball is how it affects the completion of the swing. It does not affect the short clubs too adversely (see lower photographs, first two "hitting" with premature observation; latter two "natural" with head still). The "hitting" arc is still steep and not far removed from completion of "natural". Note the disparity in completion with long clubs above (first two "hitting" with premature observation; latter two "natural" with head still).

113

SECTION 3: EVERY GOLFER SHOULD RESPECT AND FACILITATE THE INFLUENCES OF NATURAL SWINGING MOTION:

WHY OBSERVE THE BALL'S FLIGHT IMMEDIATELY AFTER IMPACT WITH THE CLUBHEAD ANYWAY?

If you think carefully about it, there is no logical reason to follow the ball's flight immediately after impact with the clubhead anyway. First and foremost, there is no point in looking at the ball with the intention to see if it is been struck squarely by the clubhead. The actual impact takes place so quickly that it is nigh to impossible to determine if the impact is square or not. The golfer will know soon after whether the impact was square by observing the flight path of the ball since this will indicate the trueness or otherwise of the swing. If the ball flies on a straight flight path, the contact was square because the swing was good; if not, the contact was not square because the swing was flawed.

Second, what is the point in following the ball's flight immediately after impact since one cannot influence the flight pattern of the ball by simply looking at it anyway? At any rate, which part of the ball's flight is most important? Surely it has to be the latter part in order to see where the ball lands? So what is the point in looking at the earlier part of the ball's flight? And one need not worry that one thinks one has to follow the flight of the ball as soon as it is struck in order to track the ball or to discern where the ball will ultimately land. You can rest assured that you should have plenty of time to observe the most important part of the flight path – the latter part - before the ball lands.

If you are using a short iron, for example, the ball should spend a considerable amount of time going up and up into the air. The follow-through/shoulder turn of the club should bring your head upwards. You should thus catch sight of the ball in the final stages of its upward flight, or at worst, at the beginning of its descent. At any rate, if the worst comes to the worst and the player looks up prematurely to observe the flight path, the "swinging" motion should not be too adversely affected since there is little swinging motion with properly swung short clubs anyway.

If you are using a longer club, the distance the ball travels through the air is greater so the ball should spend more time in the air. By the time your head has been turned by the momentum of the follow-through you should have sufficient time to catch sight of the ball at some stage as it travels through the air well before it lands on the ground. And even if you only catch sight of the ball as it lands, you should see it clearly as it runs on and on along the ground on account of its shallow descent onto the ground.

The situation is often quite ironic. Many naive golfers are keen to admire the ball's flight. Yet the very watching of the flight of the ball immediately after contact with the clubhead might mean that the flight could be far from admirable.

How the premature looking of the ball's flight can be the bane of your golf game:

The typical naive golfer who does not understand the characteristics of natural swinging motion is really in a vicious circle. The basis for the conflict between **golf sense** and **common sense** is simple. **Golf Sense** says give the clubs the *amounts* of swinging motion they require. **Common Sense** does not give *any* club the amount of swinging motion it requires. Since the shorter clubs do not require swinging motion as such, this strategy is not damaging to these clubs. But the other clubs are severely affected.

Golfers who use this **common sense** strategy are likely to have an inferiority complex, as it were, with the longer clubs on account of inconsistences they encounter with these clubs. They are more likely to observe the ball's flight prematurely because they are not fully confident that the ball will travel to its intended target. *But this very action of premature observation contributes to the failure of the ball to travel to its intended target in the first place.*

But the naïve golfer's anxieties to observe the flight of the ball prematurely can also be quite intense with the shorter clubs on occasions. They are often confronted by hazards. These hazards include bunkers on the fairway or green-side or water surrounding the greens that are within the compass of these clubs. The naive golfer who is unsure of their game at the best of times would have even greater anxiety to see where the ball goes upon impact with the clubs in these circumstances. "Hitting" action might have compensations with high-lofted clubs. But sometimes these golfers rush their action so much in their anxiety with these clubs that the strikes on the ball are not good enough. Very often the ball ends up in these hazards as a result!

And anxiety is not confined to worry. At other times, the naïve golfer wishes to propel the ball as closely as possible to the pin with a chip. They observe the flight of the ball immediately after impact with the clubhead to determine how successful their effort is. Very often the ball fails to move significantly at all. Ask yourself, how many times have you *"fluffed"* a chip and were told by your playing partners that you *"looked up"*?

Observe the professionals:

You should notice how professional golfers restrain themselves from observing the ball as soon as it leaves the clubface in still impact photographs in the sports sections of newspapers and golf magazines. You should see how their heads are still. Their eyes are focussed on a spot of ground where the ball had been located before them well after the ball has flown off after impact and the clubhead is on the follow-through.

An even better way to discern the same phenomenon can be discerned from studying video footage of these professionals as they swing the clubs. Play back the swing frame-by-frame and you should see how the head remains still once the swing has been initiated, once impact is made between ball and clubhead and once the ball leaves the clubface. You should see how the golfer's head

116

moves some time late in the follow-through.

The golfer may have restricted the movement of the head until then consciously and then moved the head personally. The golfer may have allowed the swinging motion itself to move the head. Either way, you should see how the golfer has slickly co-ordinated the natural posture of the head following the swing into a seemingly free-flowing natural observation of the ball. And this is why it appears such golfers appears to look up to observe the ball's flight immediately upon impact with the clubhead.

LESSON NO. 11:

Some golfers either restrict the movement of the head consciously and move the head personally late in the follow-through or they allow the swinging motion itself to move the head late in the follow-through of longer clubs. This ensures that they can still follow the flight of the ball and succeed in creating the natural golf swing properly because they complete the natural swinging motions of these clubs.

Another possible explanation as to why some naive golfers find it more difficult to move the ball properly with the longer clubs:

It could be argued that the only real skill in golf is the discipline to allow the swinging motion to carry out its influences. We read in the last chapter, for example, how the naïve golfer often uses their own, often indiscriminate, force to hit the ball with the club. Other golfers allow the stored force of the clubhead from its swinging motion to hit/impact the ball instead. Here we see how the naïve golfer often observes the flight of the ball prematurely and fails to complete the swinging motion in full. One should come to understand that the swing influences the golfer and does so with as much importance as the golfer's contribution to the swing itself.

Herein lies one possible explanation as to why some naïve golfers incur difficulties in moving the golf ball with the longer clubs in particular. Ideally, you see, golfers should fulfil the contradictory characteristics of swinging motion (giving them the amount of swinging motion they require and facilitating the swinging motion in turn) at the same time. This task poses little difficulties to naïve golfers who use their **common-sense** when employing "hitting" action with the shorter clubs. These shorter clubs require little swinging motion. It does not really matter if these contradictory characteristics of swinging motion are obliged at any time not to mention at the same time.

But the longer clubs require substantial amounts of swinging motion. Firstly, they require greater amounts of swinging motion than the shorter clubs. So the golfer must *contribute more* in terms of physical energy to making a long club swing properly than a shorter one. Secondly, they require the golfer to *restrain themself more* from observing the flight of the ball immediately after impact with the club. Yet the golfer's anxieties to observe the ball are likely to be greatest with these clubs. Fulfilling the contradictory characteristics of swinging motion at any time, not to mention at the same time, with the longer clubs, then, is certainly more arduous than doing so with the shorter clubs. It seems golf requires more mental resolve than physical skill!

LESSON NO. 12:

It would seem that moving the ball properly in golf demands greater levels of skill in terms of mental resolve rather than simply physical skill of its own right since one should have the discipline to allow the swinging motion to carry out its duties/influences in moving the ball and golfer's head.

GOLDEN RULE No. 3:

The golfer should position their feet/legs carefully to keep the body stable from the momentum of the swinging motion. They should either allow their heads to be moved by the momentum of the swinging motion or do not move their heads contrary to it and synchronise the movements of their heads to observe the flight of the ball. This should ensure that they complete the swinging motion of the clubs. The golfer should allow the clubhead to impact with the ball. Every golfer has to respect and facilitate the swing's influences.

SECTION 4: IT'S A MATTER OF HAVING FAITH IN THE CLUBS AND SWINGING THEM FOR SWINGING SAKE ONLY:

USING **NONSENSE** TO HELP UNDERSTAND **GOLF SENSE**:

There is one exercise that might help you overcome the anxiety to observe the ball's flight immediately after impact with the clubhead, particularly with the longer clubs. Take a cleaning mop, or any other object that has approximately the same length of a driver. Ensure that no other object gets in the way of your swinging of this object around your body a few times. Close your eyes during the entire session. Adopt relevant procedures as per some practise-swings to swing the mop naturally properly. Allow the momentum of the swinging motion of the mop to move your head. *This, for what it's worth, is the natural golf swing personified.* If you were swinging a driver and had a ball placed in front of you, it should have been propelled properly.

This is the simplicity of the natural golf swing. But for many naïve golfers, however, playing golf becomes a complicated matter. We are familiar by now how many of these golfers approach the game with the attitude of hitting the ball with the clubs with their own, often indiscriminate, force. This happens to be reasonably successful with short clubs. But it can be dogged by inconsistencies with longer ones. As a result, these golfers can become confused.

Moreover, many naïve golfers become obsessed with the competitive objective of the game, that is, the task of putting the ball in the hole with the least amount of strokes. Since these golfers approach this task with a somewhat unreliable methodology, they invariably become frustrated with their failure. This frustration, of course, simply evaporates the relaxation the mind requires to swing any club properly. So the naïve golfers end up exaggerating their hitting actions on the ball with even more disastrous results. This confusion, allied to frustration, undermines the potential of exercising the simplicity of the natural swing.

The competitive edge in other ball sports often makes competitors frustrated as well. But this does not necessarily detract them from their *enjoyment* of the game. These other ball sports are played at a faster pace and in more robust physical conditions than golf. Competitors often do not have the time to wallow in their frustrations and they have to get on with the game, often for self-protection. Taking their frustration out of the ball by hitting it as hard as they can often results in the release of their frustration. But it does not necessarily affect the trajectory of the ball in flight. Sometimes the frustrations inspire them to play more competitively. In many ways, more enjoyment is taken from these frustrations when success prevails.

Golf is played under different conditions. Repeated frustration with the golf ball is not likely to inspire the golfer to move the golf ball better if the golfer cannot understand the reasons why the ball is not being moved properly in the first place. One could be better advised, then, to distinguish the simplicity of the natural swing from the complications of playing the game of golf (competitively). Ironically, if one dispenses with the objective of the golf game and pursues the simplicity of the swing only, one is far more likely to succeed in achieving the dispensed objective in the first place. This theme is further developed in Chapter 6. This is why we have replaced the driver here with the mop.

When you have become accustomed to swinging the mop, you should place a chair or some other object very close to the follow-through path of its swinging motion. Set the object up so that the mop head barely avoids it on the follow-through. Now begin your swing. *Will you have the mental resolve to trust the swing?* In other words, will you have the confidence that the mop head will not collide with the object and therefore allow the swinging motion to move your head naturally on the follow-through? Or will you be unsure? Will you look up anxiously on the follow-through to see if the mop head collides with the object instead?

If you trust the swing and allow your head to be moved by the momentum of its swinging motion, the mop head should not collide with the object. You should be creating natural swinging motion properly. The mop head should stay in its natural flight path that you have already ensured will avoid the object. If you do not trust the swing, on the other hand, the mop head is likely to collide with the object. The forced movement of your head as you doubted the swing might throw the mop head out of its natural flight path with resulting disaster.

This exercise can also prove to you if you are employing the correct energy level to swing the mop. The mop head should not collide with the object if the energy you supply to swing it is correct. Ideally, you should progress from swinging a cleaning mop to swinging actual golf clubs themselves, with a softer object in place in case a collision does take place.

The real beauty of this exercise is twofold. Firstly, you are only using a mop. But it requires a certain amount of energy to give it its swinging motion and the swinging motion in turn needs to be catered for ... just as the golf clubs do. It does not matter what you swing naturally - the keystones of natural swinging motion have to apply. Does this mean that it might be useful to change your mindset? Should you begin to view the golf clubs as instruments to swing and not as mere implements to hit the ball with your own force with?

Secondly, did you notice the nature of the motion the mop took as you were employing it? Was it not smooth, free-flowing, fluid yet powerful? Is this the same nature of the motions the clubs take when they are used abruptly and/or aggressively? Using the mop eliminated the golfing perspective when employing the mop - a natural swinging motion with the mop accrued. Does this mean that it might be useful to eliminate the golfing perspective when employing the golf clubs. **Nonsense**......or **Golf Sense**?

IT'S A MATTER OF IGNORANCE & FEAR Vs. FAITH:

We saw earlier in Chapter 2 how "hitting" action is not likely to educate the golfer that swinging motion influences them since "hitting" action has very little swinging motion attached to it. In this chapter, we have seen how many naive golfers suffer from a lack of confidence in the longer clubs, borne by inconsistencies through their "hitting" actions on the ball. This lack of confidence calls for anxiety in prematurely observing the ball, that in turn, contributes to these inconsistencies in the first place. The misfortunate naive golfer is *"between a rock and a hard place"*.

It could be argued, then, that ignorance of the natural swing and fear of failure are the hallmarks of the typical naïve golfer's failure to move the golf ball consistently with the longer clubs. They may benefit from a thorough understanding of the natural swing and consequently affirm a stoic faith in the clubs and in the natural swing. Perhaps they should learn to accept that if the clubs are swung properly – and this entails the discipline to allow the clubhead impact the ball through its swinging motion and the discipline to allow the head to be moved by the same swinging motion of the club – then the ball has a better likelihood of being propelled properly. *It's a test of faith in the clubs and the swing.*

ADD TO ROUTINE:

Thus far, a routine of taking some practise-swings with the clubs has developed. In so doing, one is likely to create natural swinging motion of a club properly by ensuring relevant components such as correct energy levels, correct stance and correct head posture are geared to creating the natural golf swing. Furthermore, practise-swings help the golfer to become aware of the uniqueness of the characteristics of the natural swinging motion of a particular club. They acclimatise oneself, as it were, to the nuances of the characteristics of that club when taking the swing for real. The moving of the head by the swinging motion of the club should now be added to this routine.

Let's go back to the example of using the three-iron and the wedge earlier. A practise swing could be used to determine differences in how the swinging motion moves the head on the follow-through with both clubs. This is better advised once one has checked that the chin does not collide with the shoulders first so the head is free to be moved by the swinging motion in the first place (the golfer could determine correct stance and head posture from the first swing).

The wedge would have hardly moved the head at all from its insignificant swinging motion. But the swinging motion of the three-iron is accompanied by a more significant amount of swinging motion. It should thus bear some impact on moving the golfer's head. Thus, taking a practise-swing should inform the golfer of the extent of this effect on the moving of the head and fore-warn them, as it were, that it accompanies the natural swinging of that club.

All the golfer has to do on the golf course is to replicate the practise routines above in their totality in preparation for making the golf swing for real. There should have been little difficulty in creating the natural golf swing through the practise-swings. But making the swing for real brings the ball into the equation. The golfer may have the discipline to restrain themself from hitting the ball with the clubs with their own force as they look at the ball before impact. The golfer may have the discipline to restrain themself from observing the flight of the ball as soon as it leaves the clubface. If they cannot discipline themselves so, they should find a means to help them so. By the way, how did the technique of looking at a spot of ground behind the ball as you swung the clubs in the driving-range go for you earlier?

But before we go any further, there remains, however, another component *outside* the swing itself - the address - that needs to be included in our natural golf swing checklist. This is dealt with in the next chapter.

RECAPITULATION:

(i) Focussing on the ball before and during the swing before the ball is impacted has to be very disciplined. It can instil a determination to hit the ball with the clubs with one's own force at the expense of swinging the clubs naturally.

(ii) If one swung a short club naturally, one would generate little swinging motion with the club. The head would not be affected by the "swinging" motion of the club. If, however, one swung a longer club naturally, one would generate significant swinging motion with this club. This would influence the movement of the head during the follow-through stage of the swing. This is best discerned by swinging the clubs with the eyes closed.

(iii) This is how natural swinging motion influences the golfer's head as it is being completed. These influences should be allowed to take place so that natural swinging motion can be created properly through its proper initiation, sustenance and completion. Alternatively, a golfer can restrain the movement of the head consciously until late in the follow-through.

(iv) The typical naïve golfer uses "hitting" action on the ball and does not create swinging motion with the clubs. It is immaterial that their heads are not moved by the "hitting" action since this action is inappropriate to moving the ball in the first place. At any rate, the focus of the typical naïve golfer is on the ball only. Thus, they use their **common sense** to observe the ball as soon as it leaves the clubface and inevitably, the hitherto swinging motion is not completed since the focus has become the ball's flight. Proper swinging motion has not been created.

Golf Sense Vs. Common Sense.

Note similarities between swinging a mop naturally above and swinging a driver naturally below.

CHAPTER 4: COMMON-SENSE & THE PRE-SWING PRINCIPLES.

Hopefully, it is becoming apparent by this stage that some naïve golfers use their **common sense** in their attempts to move the golf ball. Their pre-occupation in trusting their **common sense** is again evident in part in the pre-swing principles, that is, the things golfers do before they actually swing the clubs. Many golf instruction books refer to these pre-swing principles at the start of their books. This book has already referred to some of these principles already in describing its cornerstone lesson (that "swinging" action is probably more reliable than "hitting" action). Now the time is appropriate to describe the outstanding pre-swing principles and to refresh ourselves on aforementioned ones.

The pre-swing principles essentially incorporate the grip and address factors such as aligning one's body parallel to the target-line; adopting a suitable posture to swing the clubs freely and without discomfort to the body; and, the position of the ball in relation to the golfer's body before the golfer swings the clubs.

The reader should never under-estimate the importance of these pre-swing principles. The golfer should learn how to address the ball properly and how to hold the club properly before they swing the clubs. After all, if you wish to fire a bullet from a rifle at an object, you should ensure that you are handling the rifle properly and that you have it pointing at that object before pulling the trigger.

Addressing the body to the ball:

Addressing the body to the ball means the position the golfer takes in relation to the golf club, their body, the golf ball and the target before commencing to swing the club. One should adopt a particular posture or *"step into"* the ball in a particular way so that the swinging motion of the clubhead is aligned to impact with the ball to send it a particular direction. To address the ball properly you should align your body parallel to the target line (the direct path the ball would take to the fairway, pin and so on).

One of the easiest ways to do this is to stand back behind the ball and note the direction you wish to propel the ball. Take note of a spot of ground some inches ahead of the ball along the target line. Then "step in" to the ball with your body being parallel to the line between the ball and the spot of ground. Place the clubhead square behind the ball. Alternatively, you can discern the target line and place the clubhead square behind the ball before "stepping in". Using a focal point to denote a target-line is common in other sports. Rugby players, for example, often pick out a particular part of a stadium behind and between the uprights as they attempt to kick the ball through the uprights.

There is one very common learning exercise you can avail of to ensure that you are standing parallel to the target-line. Place the ball on the ground and stand behind it to note the target-line. Place another golf ball on the ground some inches ahead of the ball along the target line. Stand in to the ball, place the clubhead behind the ball and prepare to swing the club. Once you feel your body is aligned parallel to the target-line and you are  ready to swing the club, place the club across the toes of both of your feet.

Now stand out of your address position. See if the direction of the club on the ground denoting the line of your stance is parallel to the target-line as denoted by both balls. Do not be surprised if the club that was placed by your toes is not parallel to the target-line because many naive golfers do not pay enough attention to this vital aspect of propelling the golf ball properly. Many naive golfers often mis-align themselves to the ball. While their swings may be successful in themselves, the ball is consequently imparted a glancing blow by the clubhead since the body is not parallel to the target-line. The ball consequently receives significant sidespin and veers away from the target.

Body posture:

Your body is parallel to the target line. The face of the clubhead is square behind the ball. Now you should adopt a posture where your body can comfortably accommodate a swinging action of the club around your body. Hopefully, by now, the reader is aware of the dangers of swinging the clubs in such a way as it discomforts the body. This may cause the body (or head) to tilt or sway. It is unlikely, in such circumstances, that the clubhead can remain in its natural flight path around the golfer's body. And remember: if the clubhead leaves its natural flight path at any stage before impact with the ball it may not propel the ball properly.

The first aspect of correct body posture relates to the correct feet posture or stance. Your experiences in the foregone practice-swinging sessions earlier should hopefully have taught you the correct stance to take with each club. Firstly, the lengths of the shafts of the clubs themselves dictate the distances you stand away from the ball - the longer the shafts the further you stand away from the ball. You should find the correct standing distance away from each club when you find that your hands which are holding the clubs go through the hitting area (just before, during and just after impacting the clubhead with the ball) pass parallel around your hips.

The length of each respective shaft also dictates how far apart your feet should be as you swing the clubs since different clubs take different flight paths when they are swung around the golfer's body. We have already seen in Chapter 2 how your feet should be most apart with the longer clubs. This is because the body needs maximum stability when the clubheads take the widest flight paths around your body. They generate significant amounts of swinging motion that is moving away from the body. The feet should be least apart when using the shorter clubs because the arcs (or "planes") are more steep than shallow and generate little swinging motion. The feet, as a result, do not have as much swaying motion to support.

The second aspect of correct body posture relates to the correct head posture (referred to earlier in Chapter 2). Remember: you should adopt a posture such that your body can comfortably accommodate a natural swinging action of the club around your body. Thus, you should ensure that your shoulders do not collide with your chin on the backswing as this collision may tilt your head. This could throw the clubhead out of its natural flight path in itself. Or it may dis-orientate you and it is likely that the clubhead will be jerked out of its natural flight path on account of the loss of your body's stability. Shoulder/chin collision, then, is really a physical obstruction to the creation of the natural golf swing rather than a flaw created in the nature of the swinging motion itself.

The key to overcoming this flaw is to take a practice swing or two to check if the shoulders do indeed collide with the chin. If they do, then you could adopt two procedures as follows. Firstly, make sure that you are not standing totally erect as you swing the clubs. If you adopt this posture it is possible that you might create a steep flight path with the clubs. This could encourage a collision between the shoulders and chin since the shoulders could be moving upwards towards your chin on the backswing. Notwithstanding this effect, we have already read how the encouragement of a steep plane with the longer clubs can also lead to uncertainity that the contact between ball and clubhead at impact will be square.

What you could do is bend your legs a little so that your body sits down somewhat, as it were, as you swing the clubs. This has the effect of moving your shoulders forward of your body (or your body back from your shoulders) so that the shoulders have more freedom to revolve around your body. This should reduce the risk of collision with your chin. You may have heard the adage *"never stand tall to the ball"*. Well now, hopefully, you understand why.

To further reduce the risk of a collision, you should tilt your chin upwards in your posture to a comfortable degree. Then take another practice swing to ensure the shoulders do not collide with the chin. If there is clearance, that is, if the shoulders stay under the chin during the backswing, then you should persist with this posture for the swing you wish to actually make when moving the ball forward. The posture may feel uncomfortable at first. But clearance between the shoulders and chin should prevail as otherwise the swing may never be a natural one. Like other aspects to your golf game, changes that you undertake might feel uncomfortable at the start. But you should become accustomed to them over time and eventually these adjustments should feel natural and instinctive to you. This should be the case if your focus becomes the creation of natural swinging motion with the clubs in particular. The only way to succeed is to practise, practise and practise again.

This flaw of non-clearance between shoulders and chin is particularly exacerbated with naïve golfers who swing the clubs too aggressively. When the head posture is incorrect, aggressive swinging is likely to increase the force of collision between shoulders and chin. And, of course, the flaw is also more likely with the longer clubs since they have most swinging motion associated with them and take the shoulders more around the golfer's body towards the chin.

The ball position:

There seems to be no one absolute rule when it comes to positioning the golf ball in relation to the golfer's stance. Some golfers place the ball forward in their stance when using the longer clubs (the woods, 3 & 4 iron), in the middle of their stance for the middle clubs (5,6,7 irons) and back in their stance with the short irons (8,9, Wedge & Sand Wedge).

The ball is usually placed forward in the stance when using the long clubs because the angle of approach with these clubs is shallow. The clubhead of a long club "sweeps" along the ground, as it were, just before, during and immediately after impact with the ball. We noted earlier how the ball requires impact more from behind the back of the ball when using the longer clubs. Thus, the forward positioning of the ball in the stance facilitates the "sweeping" movement of the clubhead forward towards the back of the ball and tries, as best as it can, to eliminate severe sidespin being imparted on the ball. The longer the club, the further forward the ball is placed in the stance. The driver occupies the furthest position with the ball in line with the toes of the left foot for right-handed golfers and the toes of the right foot with left-handed golfers. Indeed, the loft of the driver is so low that the ball requires an upward contact with the clubhead and is consequently placed on a tee peg to facilitate this ascending impact.

The middle irons are usually placed in the middle of the stance while the shorter irons are usually placed back in the stance. This placing toward the rear of the stance with the short irons reinforces the steep angle of approach of the shorter irons. The clubheads are consequently brought more down onto the back of the ball. This rear placement consequently encourages backspin with these clubs. The shorter the club, the further back it is placed in the stance with the sand wedge occupying the furthest position back in line with the heel of the right foot of the right-handed golfer (vice-versa for the left-handed golfer).

Other golfers prefer to keep the ball central between the stance with all clubs, except the driver. Keeping the ball central to the stance means it is easier for the golfer to create the swing since the body becomes the central axis around which the clubs swing. This poses few, if any, difficulties with the short or middle irons.

The situation with ball positioning can become a dilemma for the golfer with regard to the longer clubs. Keeping the ball central to the stance with a long club means that the ball is slightly back of centre in the stance since the golfer's hands are still forward of the ball at address. There is not as much forgiveness in the swing since the clubhead comes to impact the ball earlier on the downswing. Having said that, if the swing were very true, impact conditions would be very good since the ball would be receiving a downward, yet suitable, blow from the clubhead.

Having the ball positioned forward of the golfer's body gives greater forgiveness to the contact between ball and clubface. The clubhead now comes to impact the ball near to the beginning of the follow-through stage. But the golfer's hands are also forward of the golfer's body at address. The swing itself may now be more difficult to create since the central axis of this swing is not central to the golfer's body. The clubs will not be revolving around the golfer's body as a central axis as such. Furthermore, impact conditions might not be as good as a true swing in a central position since the ball would be receiving a lesser downward blow from the clubhead.

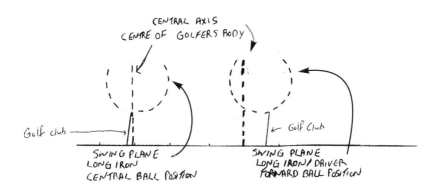

Regardless of which method of employment of force one uses, the golfer has to position the ball forward of the stance with the driver because its loft is so low. Even the natural golf swing cannot move the ball properly with the driver unless it is forward of the stance. The blow would be downward on the ball and there would not be enough loft left in the clubface to get the ball sufficiently up into the air. Thus, creating the natural swing with the driver is also somewhat more difficult since the central axis of this swing is not centered around the golfer's body.

The situation is not as exacerbated with the other "woods" unless they are being played when the ball lies on the ground. These clubs are designed to take a downward impact but it is safer to keep these clubs somewhat forward of the golfer again so that the downward impact will not be too severe.

Never underestimate the address factors:

Have no doubt about it – every experienced golfer takes tremendous consideration in setting-up to the ball properly and positioning the ball correctly before swinging the clubs. They may have their own individual way of doing these things. But none will begin the swinging motion of any club until they are confident that the pre-swing principles have been observed and respected and that they are primed consequently to create the swing.

THE GRIP:

The grip is the only physical link between the golfer and the clubs and it's importance, in general, has been highlighted earlier. The simple fact of the matter is that one cannot swing a club naturally unless one holds it in a particular way that allows it to swing in the first place. The unfortunate reality, however, is that many naive golfers do not hold the clubs to this effect. So their chances of creating the natural golf swing are severely hampered ever before they even initiate the swing.

The way the typical naïve golfer holds the clubs, you see, usually reflects their intention to hit the ball with the clubhead with their own physical strength. While one must hold the clubs with one's hands, the naive golfer literally grips the club tightly with the palms of their hands because they intend to force the clubhead onto the ball with their own, very often, indiscriminate physical force.

Our experiences in life tell us that a tight grip is often the correct way to hold objects when employing them. After all, we grip things tightly in our palms so that we can utilise them, for example, a sweeping brush or a frying pan. Players in other ball sports have to have an over-powering and wielding grip on their striking instruments because they play in a physically forceful game. Tennis players, for example, move the ball by hitting it as hard as they can on their forehand and backhand. Hockey players need a similar grip on their hockey sticks because hockey sticks often clash and collide with each other. Thus, **common sense** tells us that a wieldy grip is the correct way to hold the golf clubs since we think we should use personal force with them to move the ball.

Golf sense, however, tells us to use the force generated by the swinging of the clubs. The natural golf swing is a more reliable method of moving the ball so one might be better advised to hold the clubs to enable them to swing at least. And one can allow the clubs to swing freely with a firm yet sensitive grip using some of the fingers of the hands.

The sensitivity of the finger grip:

The reader will recall the analogy earlier between the grip a golfer exerts on a golf club with the fingers and that of an experienced jockey on the reins of his horse. Both grips allow movement. If the golfer's grip was primarily with the palms of the hands, the golfer would be exerting personal influence on the flight paths the clubs take. The finger grip thus gives greater opportunity for the clubheads to find flight paths that are natural to the golfer's physical characteristics. It also allows the clubheads to impact the ball through their swinging motions. Finally, it enhances the golfer's perception of the amount of strain it takes of them to swing the clubhead from its inception to its completion around the body. This is vital since clubs vary in length and the golfer must use only the energy required to swing each club individually.

LESSON NO. 13:

> **While it takes a different amount of energy to initiate and sustain the swinging motion of one club from another because of the variance in the length of club shafts and clubhead size/composition, in each case the golfer should only use the required amount of energy to do so.**

The firmness of the finger grip:

But while the sensitive finger grip allows the clubhead to impact with the ball, the grip itself should also be firm so that the impact should not loosen the grip from which the clubhead may not impact squarely through the ball. Furthermore, the grip should also be firm so that the clubhead will not lose its angle of clubface (presumed to be square at address) as it is swinging around the golfer's body.

Thus, we should not really refer to the grip one uses when handling a club but rather use the term *"hold"*. *"Grip"* conveys an over-powering handling of the club. One is in a position to manipulate the club to do whatever one wishes to do with the clubhead. Thus, the *"grip"* is prevalent when the intention is to hit or beat the ball with the clubs with personal force.

If you *"hold"* the club with your fingers, on the other hand, you facilitate the club's natural ability to swing. All you have to do then is to direct this swinging motion around your body and allow the clubhead to do the business of moving the ball for you. Remember – the golfer swings, the clubhead hits. The core difference is that the palm grip is powered by the wrists whereas the finger grip limits the wrists to revolve through the swinging motion only. You've probably heard *"Grip it and Rip it"*. Beware!

And a physical examination of the clubs themselves should also impress on the reader why the finger hold is more appropriate. Golf clubs are much lighter in weight than other striking instruments such as hurleys, baseball bats, cricket bats and so on. A cricket bat, for example, weighs between 2 lbs., 7 oz.- 2lbs., 12oz. while the average golf club weighs under 7 oz (6 times less). The finger grip would not have the physical strength to utilise other striking equipment effectively for the type of power they require through brute force. An over-whelming grip, on the other hand, would stifle the fluidity and rhythm of a golf club. It would never be allowed to materialise the type of power it requires through smoothness of motion. And let's not forget that the golf ball weighs a maximum of 1.6 oz while the cricket ball and baseball are approximately over 5oz.

Finally, it is no harm to stress again that the correct "hold" on any club is vital for an appropriate initiation of the swinging motion of its clubhead. Initiating the swing is the trickiest part of the swinging motion process because the clubhead lies on the ground as a lifeless object. The clubhead must go from inertia to mobility but it cannot be made to begin to move in any haphazard kind of way. The clubhead must enter a set groove - its natural flight path - as it moves around the golfer's body. Thus, one safe way to ensure that the clubhead does enter its natural flight path at the very beginning of the swing is to push the clubhead gently along the ground with the appropriate energy as gauged by sensing the strain of the clubhead through the finger grip.

THE GRIP IN MORE DETAIL:

There are a variety of recognised grip positions that are described in other golf instruction books. These books can be quite technical, for example, grip positions are defined as "weak", "strong" and "neutral" with references made to the "V's" of the thumbs and index fingers pointing to the shoulders and so on. The more conventional "grip" for right-handed golfers usually follows along the lines of the Vardon overlap grip in which the little finger of the right hand overlaps with the index finger of the left hand (vice-versa with left-handed golfers) as described in Chapter 1.

While many golf instruction books describe the theories of the various technicalities of the finger grip, they seldom, if ever, explain why the finger grip should be adopted. They are also prescriptive as to the range of stereo-typed grips from which the reader should only employ. It may be wiser for the naïve golfer to understand the principles underlying the finger grip and to experiment themselves so as to develop a grip  with the fingers that suits the individual. *Remember: all that matters is that the clubhead returns square to the ball at impact.* You should hold the clubhead square at address with whatever finger grip you feel comfortable with and continue to feel comfortable with as you swing the club around your body so that the clubhead will hopefully return square to the ball at impact.

The actual location of the hands on the handles of the clubs as one holds the clubs is also a matter of individual preference. Many golfers hold all clubs near to the top/end of the handle for standard shots. Others, however, tend to place their hands further down from the top/end of the handles as they use the longer shafted clubs. They believe this gives them greater control of these clubs. And beginner/high-handicap golfers could benefit from this technique as it does not necessarily result in a significant loss of yardage in moving the ball.

One aspect of hand location on the handles that is not a matter of individual preference is the locating of the hands upper and lower on the handles. Right-handed golfers should hold the right hand below the left. Conventionally, the right hand becomes the dominant one although other golfers use both hands equally when creating the swing. The situation is reversed with left-handed golfers.

PRACTISE IS THE SOLUTION:

No matter which method you use it certainly is a shock to the system to change one's grip primarily with the palms of the hands to a grip primarily with the fingers. Practise is the solution. Once again, one should visit the driving range. Practise the grip by swinging the short-shafted clubs first. These do not require the same firmness of grip as the longer ones as the strain to swing these clubs is lesser. Practise by using the fingers of the hands separately first and then with both hands together. Graduate, thereafter, to the longer clubs.

You should find that calluses should develop around the middle of these fingers, especially the middle fingers of the dominant hand. These take the strain of the swinging action most. Some professional golfers wear thin bandages around these parts of their fingers so the calluses are a sign of a good grip. You will know the "grip" is right when you can sense the weight of the clubhead as it revolves around your body whilst at the same time keeping a firm hold of the club.

The clubs are inanimate objects. They cannot leap into the golfer's hands and adopt the correct "grip" themselves. Nor can they square themselves to the ball at address by themselves. Only the golfer themself can do so. It's like a pilot in mid-flight who calibrates his instruments carefully before switching to autopilot – if everything is ok the plane itself can take over itself. So too, must the golfer ensure that the address and grip are correct, and if so, the physical characteristics of each swing should take care of themselves thereafter.

FINALISING THE ROUTINE:

Thus, we can add the address factors of correct body alignment and ball position to our checklist of factors for creating the golf swing naturally. It's not, of course, that these factors actually create the natural golf swing but rather, they serve it to move the ball properly.

THE DENTIST ANALOGY:

The checklist some golfers go through to ensure the natural golf swing is created properly is like a patient who nervously visits his dentist. He enters the dentist's chair gently with trepidation (the gentle take-away). He places his feet solidly on the ground to support the body (stance). Once seated on the chair, he closes his eyes with anxiety (closing the eyes). He grips the handles of the chair with his fingers tightly such is the tension (finger grip). He keeps his body rigid out of fear (stable body). He moves his head up so the dentist can examine his teeth (head posture). Once the dentist insets the needle into his mouth, it moves the patient's head (out of their shock).

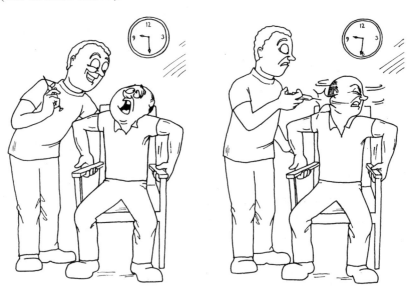

CHAPTER 5: PUTTING GOLF SENSE Vs. COMMON SENSE IN CONTEXT:

It might be helpful for the reader to discern the typical thoughts and procedures of naïve golfers who employ *"hitting"* action on the ball and those golfers who employ *"swinging"* action on the ball. It's best to compare these actions through the long clubs where disparities in success between these strategies are most pronounced. The reader may consequently recognise certain characteristics with which they may be able to identify with and from which they may determine whether they are *"hitters"* or *"swingers"*.

VISUALISING THE "HITTING"/ BEATING ACTION:

Naive golfers grip the club tightly with the palms of the hands. They consequently cannot get a *"feel"* for the clubhead to estimate the amount of energy needed to swing the club for swinging sake only. Nor do they give the clubs the opportunity to swing freely. The truth is that they rarely think about the clubhead and the natural flight path it should take. They are simply concerned with beating or hitting the ball with the clubhead in their flight path instead.

They then concentrate on the ball only. After all, this is the object they intend to hit with the clubhead with their own physical force. They do not necessarily pay sufficient attention to how the body is aligned to the target-line nor the actual positioning of the ball to them. All that matters is the ball and hitting it with the club with personal force. They might take a practise-swing with the club but this is really a gearing up to how hard they will hit the ball with the club with their own force. No checks are made for correct stance or body posture to see if the shoulders might collide with the chin.

The club is then taken-away abruptly. The clubhead is taken up or *"picked up"* off the ground by these golfers. As a result, the clubhead is not allowed to enter its natural flight path as it starts its journey around the body. They wind the forces of the club up in a rushed manner by bringing it straight behind and above the back with a strenuous physical effort. The club is not being given the amount of swinging motion it requires. The shoulders probably collide with the chin and dis-orientate the balance. The body has probably swayed from the aggressive "swinging" of the club anyway. Such golfers are not concerned. After all, their focus is on hitting the ball and this, in their mind, requires a substantial amount of force on their behalf since the ball has a long distance to travel. It does not concern them what this strenuous effort does to their body - all that matters is what the strenuous force does to the ball.

They then unwind the club forcefully in another aggressive downswing motion that resembles a short cut from the top of the backswing along a straight path to the ball. This literal "downswing" motion is again rushed since they believe the ball requires a forceful blow to send it on its way. Their body sways even more from the rushed, aggressive action. Not surprisingly, the club has no chance whatsoever of entering what should be its natural flight path towards the stationary ball. They succeed in hitting the ball with the clubhead but the angle of approach is not appropriate to make a suitable, square contact between ball and clubhead. The clubhead is not allowed to move the ball through the "swinging" motion.

Their focus, as they employ the club, is on the ball all the time since their intention is to hit it with the clubhead with their own indiscriminate force. As soon as they strike the ball with the clubhead they look up to see where it is going. They are not overly concerned with the clubhead anymore. The "swinging motion" ceases short of completion and the quick, upward head movement is contrary to what it should have been from the swinging motion itself. The "swinging" motion is not allowed to influence the moving of the golfer's head.

The body ends up in a destabilised position. The ball,

142

invariably, fails to reach its target. These naive golfers are so intent on hitting the ball with the club with their own physical force that they treat the club, in effect, as if it were a stick to simply beat the ball forward. The nature of the motions of the club is abrupt, forced and aggressive. That does not empower the club to swing naturally or create swinging motion of the club for swinging sake only – it is a hitting action with the club forced upon the ball with the express intention to move it.

VISUALISING THE NATURAL SWINGING MOTION:

Other golfers hold the club primarily with the fingers. This "grip" facilitates the club's ability to swing and affords such golfers an opportunity to get a "feel" for the weight of the clubhead in relation to the length of the club they are using. Thus, they are in a good position to gauge or estimate the amount of energy required only to initiate and sustain the swinging motion of the club to completion.

These golfers "step into" the ball properly and align the body parallel to the target-line. They take a practise-swing or two with the club to understand the nuances of the motions the club takes. They adjust the stance and head posture accordingly. The swinging motion is initiated by gently pushing the clubhead along the ground. The clubhead enters (or is allowed to enter) its natural flight path as it goes around the body. The swinging motion is sustained by sensing the clubhead as it swings around the golfers' body unhindered. The golfers continue to swing smoothly by maintaining the correct amount of energy or rhythm throughout until the swing is completed. The correct rhythm ensures that the clubhead is swung effortlessly throughout. No other force will interfere with the flight path of the clubhead as it goes around behind the body and then around again in front of the body. The golfer is giving the club the amount of swinging motion it requires.

The upper body naturally stays comfortable throughout and remains firm and rigid without strain. The clubhead returns square upon impact with the ball and "hits" it properly. The clubhead is allowed to move the ball through its swinging motion. These golfers either allow the swinging motion to move the head or restrain the head movement themselves until late in the follow-through and continue to swing the club until the swinging motion ceases naturally. Either way, they are in a position to follow the flight of the ball to its intended target. The stance remains firm and solid.

These golfers do not employ the club with the intention to hit the ball with the clubhead by using their own physical indiscriminate force. They swing the club for the sake of swinging it only. They give the club the amount of swinging motion it requires. They keep the upper-body stable throughout and adopt a suitable head posture so the swinging motion cannot be interfered with. The motions of the club are smooth and fluid and are allowed to move the ball and golfers' head. While the hitting action could be described as "force without feel", the golf swing could best be summarised as "feel without force".

Well, are you a "hitter" or a "swinger"? Do you inflict the club onto the ball with brute force to move it? Or do you employ a smoothness of motion with the club and allow this motion to move the ball instead? Are you concerned about the ball only, where it is and where it has to go? Or are you concerned with creating a natural swinging motion with the club instead which happens to move the ball and your head on the follow-through?

Every golfer rationalises quite correctly that they should use the force of the clubhead's impact on the ball to send the ball to the target. The naive golfer concludes from this to hit the ball with the club with their own force. Other golfers swing the club and allow its force, as generated through the swinging motion of the club, to impact the ball instead. Golf is a game of precision. What matters most is that the contact between ball and clubhead is square. This is unlikely to happen if one uses excessive energy when employing the clubhead to the ball as in the case of " hitting" action.

Arcs of clubs with width and depth incorporated

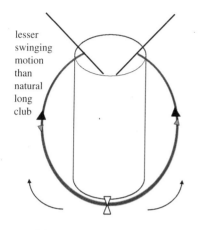

lesser swinging motion than natural long club

Short club "natural" arc.

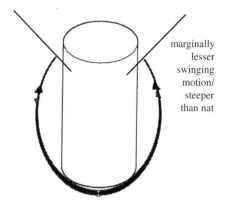

marginally lesser swinging motion/ steeper than nat

Short club "hitting" arc.

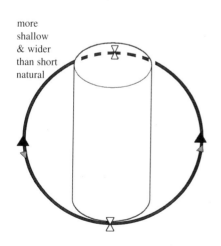

more shallow & wider than short natural

Long club "natural" arc.

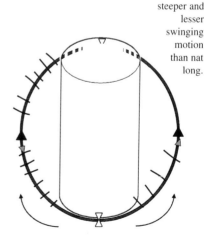

steeper and lesser swinging motion than nat long.

Long club "hitting" arc.

Note similarity in steepness of short club natural swing (left) and "hitting" action (right).

Note similarity in amount of swinging motion of short club natural swing (left) and "hitting" action (right).

Note "hitting" action with long club (right) stops earlier on backswing than does natural long club natural (left) on account of golfer's rush to hit the ball.

CHAPTER 6: HOW COMMON SENSE OFTEN COMPLICATES A SIMPLE TASK:

THE SIMPLICITY OF THE NATURAL SWING APPLIES TO GOLF IF IT IS APPLIED PROPERLY:

One should realise that the introduction and development of the game of golf did not create the concept of the swing. The swing – the bane of many golfers' life - has been with us since time began. It is a simple phenomenon. You can be sure that prehistoric man  swung a few clubs of his own to bring back uncooked dinner to the cave. The Romans used the principle of the swing when constructing huge catapults such as the *ballista* to hurl boulders at their enemy. Pendulum clocks in the mid 1600's used the swinging of the pendulum to keep the time accurately.

The origins of golf are controversial and well debated. One version points to a Scottish shepherd who swung his crook to hit pebbles whilst tending his sheep. The swing plays an intrinsic part in our lives everyday. Everyone at some stage swings something. The swing is so instinctive, natural and uncomplicated that we never actually think about it or analyse it. We have come to accept swinging motion for what it is – a simple concept. And this acceptance of its simplicity can often be the downfall of many naive golfers.

Attempting to employ the natural swing:

The typical naïve golfer often does not swing the clubs properly even if they attempt to swing the clubs naturally. This is because they think that the way that we employ everyday, ordinary swings can be applied to the natural golf swing. How often do we personally intervene with natural swings? How often, for example, do we open a door abruptly? How often do we push a child's swing-chair aggressively? We have already seen how these are natural swings in their own right that revolve around a central stable source.

But abrupt action at the beginning of a natural swing or during the sustenance of a natural swing is likely to destabilse that stable, central source. Therefore, the object that was swinging in a flight path around the source as dictated by the physical characteristics of that source (natural to that source) cannot continue on this flight path because the physical characteristics of the source have changed. The consistency in the flight path has disappeared. Not alone is the swing not natural anymore – it is as if it was never natural because it loses its fluidity and power.

The reality is that life very often places little social obligation upon us to perform everyday natural swinging actions properly. We are rarely in a position, then, to comprehend its unique but simple characteristics. The natural golf swing contains the basic elements of ordinary, everyday swings. But using only the energy required to swing the golf club gives it its naturalness. This naturalness empowers fluidity in its motion to create consistency in the power it generates. This naturalness empowers fluidity in its motion to also create consistency in the flight paths such motion takes. And consistency in power and flight paths are vital to the golfer. The golf ball has to be moved a set distance to a set target. So the natural swinging motion of the golf clubs (the natural golf swing) is a suitable means of moving the golf ball to such destinations since their design is compatible to this employment of the clubs. Rushed or forced or abrupt or aggressive actions in employing the clubs to the ball are likely to be less suitable.

Using **common sense** instead of the natural swing:

To create the natural golf swing properly, one should firstly employ the energy required only to swing each and every golf club. Each clubhead can then eventually approach the ball suitably from its natural flight path to impact it properly. This gives the swing its fluidity and power. The amount of energy required to swing one club is different to that required to swing another club because the clubs, generally speaking, have different lengths of shaft. So the golfer should determine the appropriate amount of energy to use in each case. Some golfers do this by employing an appropriate finger grip to sense the strain on the club and by swinging the club for swinging sake only a few times in practice.

What the typical naive golfer invariably does, however, is to use an excessive or haphazard amount of energy over and above that amount that is required only to simply swing the clubs naturally. They use their own indiscriminate physical strength to beat or hit the ball with the clubs instead. These excessive energy levels cannot create a natural swinging motion of the clubs around the golfer's body. The fluidity of the swinging motion is hampered and its power and consistency of motion is never established properly. Hopefully, the practise-swinging sessions have shown the reader how swinging motion generates power more appropriately than that "generated" by indiscriminate personal force instead.

Secondly, not alone should the golfer create fluidity in the swinging motion of the club to generate power, they should harness this power properly. Thus, the golfer should allow the clubhead to impact with the ball because the clubhead has the power of the swinging motion, not the golfer. Furthermore, the golfer should allow the swinging motion itself to influence the golfer if that is its perogative.

The typical naive golfer, on the other hand, uses their own personal force to move the ball with the clubs instead. They invariably move the head up to observe the ball as soon as it leaves the clubface and fail to complete the swinging motion of the club. These actions are contrary to how natural swinging motion itself should have been allowed to exert its influences. Thus, their actions dis-respect one of the keystones under-pinning the principle of natural swinging motion that can be applied to golf/golf clubs.

How can the principle be served in such circumstances? How can one then avail of the opportunities that natural swinging motion of the clubs offers to the golfer?

<u>How confusion gives suspicion to the swing:</u>

What confuses the naïve golfer is that generally speaking any kind of striking action suffices reasonably successfully with the shorter clubs. They do not require swinging motion as such. Thus, the naïve golfer is hardly likely to associate swinging motion with the other clubs. But the long clubs require swinging motion. So some naive golfers encounter difficulties with these clubs when they employ "hitting" action with them.

Thus, an overall sense of puzzlement and confusion makes them think that a great degree of skill must be required to propel the ball properly. How then, can they accept the advice that all they have to do is to swing the clubs for swinging sake alone? How can they accept that their heroes – the professionals – are frauds, as it were, because their vaulted "skill" is simply the swinging of the clubs? The last thing they are going to believe is that the simple technique of swinging the clubs naturally around their bodies is the answer to their problems.

And, of course, it is not. Natural swinging motion as it pertains to golf is a little more involved than simply the clubs in this way (keeping the body stable, correct stance/head posture, allowing the swing to move the ball and golfer's head etc..). But the fact remains that the swing in its simplicity lies at the core of the natural golf swing. Their rejection of the concept leaves them desperately seeking an alternative and often inappropriate solution to moving the ball properly.

HOW PRE-CONDITIONING COMPLICATES THE TASK OF MOVING THE BALL FOR THE TYPICAL NAIVE GOLFER:

Thus, one reason why some people are sceptical to believe that the swing can apply to the "skilled" game of golf is because people generally have become pre-conditioned to act and react in complicated ways. In our everyday lives and sporting pastimes we use non-standardised, complex and complicated actions. Life – as we well know it – is a complicated business and our actions often reflect this. When we push a sweeping-brush, for example, we are not unduly concerned about using the precise amount of force required to do so (see p. 54).

When we participate in ball sports outside of golf we are usually under some form of pressure which complicates our attitudes and reactions to striking the ball. An opponent, for example, may try to hinder our striking of the ball. The ball may be moving so that we have to adjust our striking action on it. Indeed, it is this very characteristic of non-golf ball games – its complications - which attract us to it. The complications require for a certain type of response – we call it skill. We wish, for example, that we could score goals in World Cup Finals since it is particularly difficult to do so. We consequently idolise those who do.

And it is the *manipulation* of the striking equipment that denotes the "skill" a player uses to send the ball in a certain direction in other ball sports. Let's take the situation a batsman faces in cricket. His striking instrument – the bat – is literally a blunt piece of timber. His task, to the unsuspecting observer, is to strike a ball that has been thrown at him by an opponent with this piece of timber.

This task, however, is far more complex than what it seems to be. Firstly, the ball is not simply thrown ("bowled") gracefully at the batsman in a straight-forward manner. The ball often travel at speeds of between 80-90 m.p.h. to which he only has milliseconds to react to. His opponent also puts tremendous spin on the ball as well so that it changes direction violently upon hitting the ground just before him. He must now react to this sudden change of direction and attempt to strike the ball. If he does not do so the ball may strike the wicket behind him and then he's "out" (

forced to retire). And it's not as if he can strike the ball carelessly into any direction with his bat – which in itself is not designed specifically to send the ball in any particular direction because it is essentially a blunt piece of timber. No - he must send the ball into a particular direction so that none of his opponents can catch the ball before it lands on the ground or else he is "out" again. What about tennis players who have to return serves at speeds of up to 130 m.p.h or baseball batters who face a hurtling, spinning ball at speeds of between 70-90 m.p.h? What about ice hockey players and so on who have to score despite the hampering efforts of

their opponents? And you thought hitting a stationery golf ball without any external pressures in a certain direction was difficult???

The point of this chapter is that golf is not as difficult as any other ball game from a physical point of view. But for many players golf becomes a more difficult sport to play on account of a particular mindset to the game. *They make the movement of the ball a much more complicated matter than what it really is.* The situation is quite ironic. We appreciate the "skill" a player displays when they use their judgement and reflexes in manipulating the striking equipment in other ball sports. The player has to personally influence the striking equipment in a particular way. In golf, the "skill", as it were, is not to influence the striking equipment at all other than swinging them for standard shots!!!

If there is an element of "skill" in playing golf it lies with the short game. But even at that the principle of the natural golf swing often holds true. When a golfer is faced with a chip of 40 yards what can they do since they cannot use any club fully? The golfer now needs to exercise some form of judgement in manipulating a club to execute the shot. But the manipulation of the club does not have to be brought about by physically manoevouring the club itself as in other ball sports. The manipulation is in judging how much to swing the club, perhaps half swinging a wedge to do so. And no matter how much they decide to swing the club the same principles regarding how to swing the club naturally apply.

And consider the effects of manipulating the golf clubs when moving the ball for standard shots. In other ball sports, for example, players are very often so physically pressurised by their opponents (for example, to dispossess in football) or by the physical limitations of the playing surface (end-lines, side-lines and so on) that they are compelled to change, adapt or manipulate their method of propelling the ball with their striking equipment. These players have become accustomed to striking or hitting the ball out of necessity rather than out of leisure primarily on account of these physical restrictions/pressures. In other words, they are rarely in a position whereby they could utilise their striking equipment (even if it's their hands or feet) fully, completely naturally and freely without duress.

And "hitting" the golf ball with the clubhead is a manipulation of the golf club. Consider, if you will, if you were in a position whereby you could swing your golf club fully and completely naturally without any interfering pressures. Surely the ball would travel further than it would have done if the force applied to propel the ball had been broken, jerky, stab-like, non-fluid or non- free flowing ("hitting" the ball with the clubhead with one's abrupt or aggressive physical strength)?

THE AGGRESSIVE, CONFRONTATIONAL ATTITUDE:

Another reason why the typical naïve golfer often fails to swing the clubs properly is because of another particular mindset they have when swinging the clubs. Other ball games are made difficult by elements external to the players, for example, the harassment of opponents in terms of winning possession of the ball and so on. These conditions ask for physical skills in response but also provoke a particular type of mental response. The enemy is outside and needs to be addressed from an aggressive, almost confrontational perspective. For naive golfers, the primary difficulty in playing golf is an internal one. They approach the game with a questionable attitude that often provokes them to adopt the same aggressive, confrontational approach to the ball.

Inconsistency in moving the ball properly plagues the typical naïve golfer. When the ball fails to obey, it becomes a source of anger and frustration. If the ball disobeys repeatedly, the naïve golfer becomes increasingly irritated by it. The ball becomes the enemy. The naïve golfer invariably loses the composure needed to swing the clubs naturally. Remember your practice-swinging sessions to date. When you swung the clubs with your eyes closed, did you not swing the clubs casually, freely and within your physical abilities? Did you not remain composed and relaxed throughout? Otherwise you would not have used the energy required only to swing the clubs because swinging the clubs for swinging sake only is a simple, unhurried process. So once the naïve golfer becomes frustrated with poor ball trajectories, the likelihood is that the composure required to swing the clubs naturally evaporates.

Finally, the aggressive attitude is also encouraged by the "macho" attitude of many typical naïve golfers. Power seems to be the most important thing to them. This notion, of course, takes its genesis from their watching of professional players who do indeed send the ball very long distances. Many naïve golfers swing their clubs aggressively because they think that moving the ball greater distances than fellow-players is a sign of golfing prowess. Indeed, some buy expensive clubs for further effect. How many times do you over-hear such golfers boast that they took a driver and an eight-iron at the tenth, for example, stressing that it was only an eight-iron?

Other golfers suffer no such foolishness. They know that accuracy is more important than power. They know that a particular club will send the ball a particular distance when swung properly. They know that there is no point in "swinging" a lesser club aggressively simply to show off and boast about it later. Why? Because invariably the clubhead will fail to return square to the ball and impact the ball incorrectly. And what's there to boast about if the ball veers off course violently anyway! Ironically, all naïve golfers have to do is swing their (expensive) clubs and the ball should be moved substantial distances accurately. You can buy the clubs but you cannot buy the swing. The clubs come to you ready-made to move the ball. You must make the swing.

"BUT ISN'T THE SWING A SWING?"

Many people doubt that the swing is a reliable method of propelling the ball properly. They might argue that if the clubhead is swung around the golfer's body the contact it makes with the ball can only be brief. If that is the case, the square contact it makes with the ball (if any!) must be even briefer still. How come the natural swinging motion is a reliable method of propelling the ball then?

Well, the actual contact between the clubhead and the ball may be brief. But the clubhead actually travels in a straight path just before it meets the ball when the angle of approach is satisfactory. Consequently, the swinging action has a better chance of making square contact  with the ball than the hitting action that, more likely than not, has an over-angled approach to the ball. Furthermore, the clubhead continues to travel along this straight path as it impacts the ball and for some short time thereafter. One way of describing this straight line is to take a dining plate, which when tilted, mirrors the arc of a swing. Place the plate, tilted and on its edge, on a table. The plate will rest on the table because there is sufficient "straightness" on the edge to do so. So too, does the swing contain a straight line immediately before, during and after the clubhead impacts with the ball.

RE-VISIT THE NATURAL GOLF SWING AGAIN:

An experienced golfer takes any golf club in hand and instinctively reacts, *"All I have to do is to swing this club naturally and not worry about the distance this ball has to travel."* Take out the practice clubs and swing them naturally again. Close your eyes as you swing so that your mind can register your actions and reactions to the motions of the natural golf swing. Can you differentiate between your contribution to the swing and the swing's influences over particular parts of your body? Can you sense the fluidity of the motions of the natural swings? Can you sense the power and consistency of motion through the fluidity of the motions of the natural swings?

Do not rush this familiarisation process. You should understand both sets of characteristics of the natural golf swing. You should not be in awe of them. You should and can feel so comfortable with this type of (swinging) motion that you can always be confident as to how easy it is to create the natural golf swing properly. Surely you are now beginning to realise that you can create the natural golf swing as well as any other person on the planet? The natural swing is your swing and is as good as anyone else's natural swing. Your physical ability to create the natural swing is not in question. **Your mental ability is.**

The real test is whether or not you employ the correct amount of energy to swing the club by discerning this amount from practise-swings. And whether you allow the natural swinging of the clubheads, of long clubs in particular, to move the ball and to move your head (or restrain such movement yourself in the follow-through) so that the swinging motion can be completed. When these are carried out correctly, the natural golf swing evolves.

156

CHAPTER 7: USING NONSENSE TO UNDERSTAND GOLF SENSE

THE DANGERS OF OBSERVING THE BALL:

If one was to use one's logic in the context of the golf game, one might make a startling, if not non-sensical, realisation. One could theoretically speculate that one factor that undermines the naive golfer's ability to swing the clubs naturally may be their observation of the ball during the swinging of the club itself. In Chapter 2, for example, we saw how looking at the ball could encourage one to employ *"hitting"* action on the ball with the clubs. Chapter 3 described how the completion of the natural swinging motion could be affected by the observation of the ball's flight path as soon as it leaves the clubface.

Many golfers understand the characteristics of natural swinging motion. They are able to look at the ball during the entire swinging process and reject any "hitting" thoughts. They can look at the ball and initiate and sustain the swing with the appropriate energy and not be tempted to bring the clubhead onto the ball with their own force. They have tremendous levels of discipline to restrain themselves from observing the ball as soon as it leaves the clubface to allow the swinging motion to influence their heads' movement (or restrain such movement themselves instead). *What these golfers have, in essence, is complete and utter faith in the concept of the natural swing.* Thus, they concentrate on making the swing only with the clubs and discipline themselves to comply within its physical remits. Regardless of how illogical or non-common sensible these remits seem to be.

It's reasonable to assume that not all people can have these high levels of concentration and discipline. Given the nature of the golf game where the ball is everything, one is instinctively drawn in to observing the ball. But does one have to observe the ball as one swings the clubs? Would this strategy eliminate the dangers of an abrupt take-away, aggressive sustenance of the swing and failure to complete the swinging motion through observing the ball as soon as it leaves the clubface? *Would this strategy ensure that your actions on the club are not abrupt, forced or aggressive and that you would allow the clubhead to impact the ball to move and allow it to move your head on the follow-through if that is its perogative?*

THE REASONING AND STRATEGY BEHIND NOT LOOKING AT THE BALL BEFORE, DURING AND AFTER THE SWING:

Put yourself back into the practise-swinging sessions in the driving-range. You have chosen a club you know is suitable to move the ball the required distance, you have addressed the ball properly and you are about to commence the swing.

You can, if you choose, simply decide not to look at the ball at all. What difference will it make? The ball can go nowhere until it is impacted with the clubhead. The club can only move the ball to the target once it is swung. Nobody is going to interfere with you as you attempt to swing the clubs. Think about this carefully. When you consider the playing conditions of the golf game a certain logic arises:

What can primarily stop you from swinging the club naturally other than the focus on the ball? This focus might trigger thoughts to hit the ball with the club with your own, possible indiscriminate, force and observe the flight of the ball prematurely. And you can *theoretically* overcome this pitfall by not looking at the ball at any stage of the swing since the ball plays no role in the physical creation of the swing anyway.

Thus, once a golfer has settled into the correct address position, is confident that they have chosen the correct club and is primed to make the swing, they could then focus on a spot of ground behind the ball that runs along the target-line. This – not the ball – *could* become the centre of the golfer's attention.

Theoretically, the golfer now has no compulsion to take the clubhead away **abruptly** because the ball should not be in view. The mind should be absolved of any "hitting" thoughts. *There is no ball to hit!*

The golfer continues to swing the club with the correct rhythm because, once again, *theoretically,* there should be no "hitting" thoughts distracting them from doing otherwise. There should be no ball to hit. So the golfer should simply continue to swing the club within their physical capacities. The golfer should be swinging the club **rhythmically, not aggressively**, since the golfer's eyes are focused throughout on that spot of ground behind the ball. The golfer's body should theoretically remain firm and stable. Why should a spot of ground behind the ball inspire a golfer to swing a club aggressively?

The golfer continues to swing the club and eventually the clubhead happens to impact with the ball. This should not concern the golfer. They should not even be watching the ball as it has been impacted. They should be still focused on that spot of ground behind the ball. What should have happened, in effect, is that the golfer should have **allowed the clubhead to hit the ball with the appropriate force that was generated through the swinging motion of the club.** *If all of this happens, the golfer would not be committing the first cardinal error of hitting the ball with the clubhead with their own, possibly inappropriate, force.*

The golfer continues to swing the club after impact. Any influence that the swinging motion would have on the golfer should now be able to take place. The golfer is vulnerable to such influences, as it were, because they should be still focused on that spot of ground behind the ball. If the swinging motion is quite substantial, **the golfer's head should be moved as a natural consequence of this significant force** (alternatively, the golfer may move the head consciously some time late in the follow-through). When the swinging motion of the clubhead is actually completed (nothing now should prevent the completion of the swing), the golfer's head should have been moved around their body so that they should be able to discern the latter part of the ball's flight and see where it lands. *If all of this happens, the golfer would not be committing the second cardinal error of failing to complete the swinging motion of the club through premature observation of the ball.*

Thus, a golfer could *theoretically* concentrate on a spot of ground behind the ball that could dispel any thoughts, conscious or unconscious, of dis-respecting the principles of natural swinging motion with the clubs. *Looking at the ball could focus the golfer's mind on hitting the ball indiscriminately with the clubs with their own force. Not looking at the ball could allow the golfer to swing the clubs for swinging sake only!* It could be argued that many golfers swing the clubs naturally because they see nothing to hit them with. The typical naive golfer hits the ball with the clubs with their own force because all they see is the ball and the distance it has to moved to – by hitting it.

The practice-swinging sessions you undertook with your eyes closed should also testify to the relevance of this strategy. Was this another exercise in **nonsense**? Do you not realise now that when you swung the clubs in these sessions with your eyes closed that you probably swung the clubs within your physical capabilities? If you were not focussing on the *ball,* what could have triggered "hitting" thoughts with the clubs? The ball was not there at all! Why should you have taken the clubhead away abruptly if there was no need to? After all, there was no ball to be seen and hit. You should have sustained the swing properly for the same reason. You should have completed the swing because nothing, the premature observation of the *ball,* for example, should have prevented you from doing so. If you were observing a golf ball throughout you may have stretched your body to the limit in the effort to hit the ball as hard as you could. This could have become "hitting" action on the ball with uncertain outcomes.

And let's not forget that you were advised to implement this strategy in practise-swinging sessions throughout the book already. How did it go for you? Perhaps your experience in these particular sessions provide your interpretation of the **nonsense** or otherwise of this strategy. You may have found the strategy useful. You may have not. Have no doubt about it, the theory works - it is the practical implementation or sturdiness of change of mindset that accompanies it that matters.

A TESTING DEVICE

Another advantage of focussing on a spot of ground behind the ball as you swing the clubs is that the spot of ground can act as a testing device to determine whether or not you are swinging the clubs too aggressively. This is particularly relevant when using the longer clubs, especially the driver. After all, one is most likely to swing these clubs aggressively. The next time you use the driver and employ the "no-ball" technique, try to note if your eyes stay focussed on the spot of ground as the backswing comes to its end. If they do, then you are not swinging the club dangerously aggressively. If your eyes manage to stay focussed on the spot of ground then your head must be remaining stable (yet may be rotating). If, however, your eyes cannot stay focussed on the spot of ground as the backswing comes to its end, the head has been tilting. You can rest assured that the clubhead will be thrown out of its natural flight path and difficulties will arise.

USING THE TECHNIQUE TO UNDERSTAND THE NATURAL GOLF SWING RATHER THAN CREATING IT:

The change of mindset is a long and difficult road and for many people the practical implementation of the "no-ball" technique may prove too arduous. This book does not advocate that one must use the technique to create the natural golf swing on the golf course. But it can always be used to *understand* the nature of the natural golf swing off it.

161

The best way to embrace this strategy is to do so slowly over a period of time. It is best to begin with the putter for several reasons. First, it is easiest to become accustomed to learning how not to look at the ball during the swing with the putter because its swinging motion does not move your head anyway. Secondly, one can practice the technique at home in one's own time and leisure. Thirdly, the distance the ball is going to travel is going to be quite small in relation to the distances the ball travels with other clubs. You should feel more confident about not looking at the ball as you swing the putter because you can realise yourself that the ball is hardly going to be lost. On the other hand, it is quite possible that your partner will think that you have lost your sanity!!

It might be noted, in passing, that while there are multitudes of putting techniques, the putt - the single most important stroke in golf – should be viewed as a mini-swing. You line up the ball to the hole and swing the putter on a minuscule scale. If the swing is true, the ball will travel in a straight line towards the hole. Many good golfers treat the putt as a mini-swing and do not lift their heads until well after the ball has been struck.

Take out your putter at home, line the ball up to a target and practice the "no-ball" strategy. Pick a spot on the carpet ahead of the ball that is in the target line. Place the head of the putter behind the ball using this spot of carpet as a guide to the target. When you are confident that you are ready to "hit" the ball with the putter, focus on a spot of carpet behind the ball. Now swing the putter whilst looking at this spot of carpet behind the ball throughout until the swinging motion of the putter ceases. Now look up to see where the ball has gone. Do not be surprised if the ball reaches the target. Whether it did or did not, what did you notice about the motion of the putter as you employed it? Was this motion smooth and fluid? Did it take much energy to employ? Was the nature of the motion different to that you normally employ with the putter? How well can you adjust to not looking at the ball as soon as it leaves the face of the putter?

When you have become confident with the putter you should graduate to the short irons. Remember your objective is to discern the essence of the natural golf swing: what is the nature of the type of motions the clubs take as you employ them with no thoughts of the ball in mind? How does the swinging motion influence you in turn?

Ideally, you might practice the technique in your garden if it is big enough. Start with the sand wedge. Swing the club with whatever amount of swinging motion the boundaries of your garden can accommodate. Practice the strategy of lining up the ball to the target with a patch of ground ahead of the ball. When you are ready to swing, focus on a spot of ground behind the ball that is a continuation of the target-line. Forget about the ball - discern the nature of the motions of the clubs as you swing them and what influence, if any, the swinging motions have on you. If the motions are true natural swinging ones, the ball should travel to its target. If the ball travels to its target, were the motions of the clubs smooth and fluid yet influential on you? It is all a matter of practice. The more you practice the more confident you should become with the strategy. And have no doubts about it – you can swing the clubs properly by not looking at the ball as you attempt to do so.

Thereafter, you will probably have to go to the driving range to practice with the remaining short irons and middle irons. Never move on to the next club until you have become confident that you could swing the present club without looking at the ball and have discerned the nature of the motions the clubs take and other influences.

The real test of your mental resolve, of course, comes with the longer clubs. Will you have the mental fortitude to remain with the simple swinging of the clubs for swinging sake only even though the ball has to be moved substantial distances? Will your employment of these clubs be such that the clubs will move smoothly and rhythmically around your body as natural swinging motions should do? Will you contain your anxiety to observe the ball as soon as it leaves the clubface and allow the swinging motion to move your head on the follow-through instead? Or will you fail? Will you look up to observe the ball as soon as it leaves the clubface? Will you return to abrupt and aggressive actions with the clubs to force the clubhead onto the ball to move it instead?

You will not return to these hazardous preoccupations if you have the mental strength to stay focussed on that spot of ground behind the ball throughout. In these circumstances you will have nothing to hit the clubs with with your own force. When one intends to hit the ball with the club, you see, the ball becomes the focal point for the naïve golfer. *The golfer's approach revolves around the ball.* So if the ball did not exist in the golfer's mind it might eliminate the intention to use the club as a hitting instrument – it might allow the golfer to swing the clubs for swinging sake only instead. Your actions with the clubs should now be natural - you should be making the natural golf swing and noting its smooth and fluid nature of motion. This is the purpose of this "nonsensical" exercise.

When we used the "nonsensical" notion of keeping the eyes closed in the practise-swinging sessions in the very beginning, we hoped it would help us to create and understand the natural golf swing. When we used the "nonsensical" notion of employing the mop in Chapter 3, we wondered if removing the golfing perspective when using the clubs might be beneficial. This time we have used the golf clubs and removed the golfing perspective in another "nonsensical way". Have any of these exercises in **nonsense** shown you the differences between "swinging" and " hitting" action?

Does this suggest how careful one should tread when using **common sense** when playing golf?

CHAPTER 8: MAKING SENSE OF IT ALL:

GOLF SENSE Vs. COMMON SENSE:

When one uses one's **common sense** to hit or beat the golf ball with the clubs with one's own force, one is dictating the flight path the clubhead takes as it approaches the ball before impact. The approach may or may not be suited for the actual contact between clubhead and ball at impact. On the other hand, when one swings a club, one allows its clubhead to travel on its natural flight path around the golfer's body. This gives a greater likelihood that the approach will be suited for the actual contact between clubhead and ball at impact. This is **golf sense**.

The naïve golfer often exacerbates the **common-sense** approach above by thinking that the harder one hits the ball, the further it moves. This principle applies to the moving of the golf ball as long as the clubhead impacts the ball squarely to move it to the desired target. But a rushed or forced action by the naïve golfer to begin the swing is likely to result in the clubhead failing to enter its natural flight path in the first place. And a similar type of action with the club therafter is likely to destabilise the golfer's body at some stage and will likely jar the clubhead out of its natural flight path. In either case, the chances are increased that the clubhead will not return square to the ball at impact to move it to its intended direction.

This tendency to rush or force the clubhead onto the ball is most prevalent with the longer clubs. The naïve golfer is concerned with the greater force they think they must supply to move the ball long distances. And, of course, it is not the golfer who should impart their personal force onto the ball with the long club to move it (**common sense).** It should be the clubhead that moves the ball forward when it impacts the ball as it is being swung. Indeed, the swinging motion of the club is likely to give the clubhead both the power it requires to move the ball a desired distance and a greater opportunity for the clubhead to return square to the ball at impact to send it to its desired target (**golf sense**).

"Hitting" action often confuses the naive golfer. When this is employed on the shorter clubs, their flight paths co-incidentally resemble the steep flight paths of properly swung shorter clubs. They invariably send the ball to its intended target. Naturally swung longer clubs, on the other hand, take shallow flight paths around the golfer's body. These clubs take steep flight paths when golfers intend to hit the ball with these clubs with their own force. Furthermore, the rhythm of properly swung long clubs is slower than that of properly swung shorter clubs since the longer clubs take wider flight paths around the golfer's body (**golf sense**). Yet the naïve golfer very often uses their **common sense** in thinking that the longer clubs should be "swung" as quick, if not even quicker, than shorter clubs because the distance the ball should travel is greater. The naive golfer's actions are consequently likely to account for poor contact conditions between ball and clubhead at impact.

First, these steep angles of approach are not suited to the low lofts of longer clubs that require impact from a shallow angle of approach. Enough loft may not remain on the clubface to move the ball properly. Second, it is likely that when the naive golfer "swings" the long clubs quickly, that the clubhead of the long club is not being given the time it requires to return square to the ball at impact. Alternatively, the clubhead could be thrown out of its natural flight path. The clubhead, then, is unlikely to be square just before impacting the ball.

Indeed, the very fact that the flight arcs of short clubs have very little swinging motion at all often accounts for the naïve golfer's failure to recognise that swinging motion is actually required with the other clubs. Since the naive golfer is reasonably pleased with the outcomes of the shorter clubs, they invariably persist with the same method of employment with the longer clubs.

The naïve golfer also under-estimates how the power generated through the swinging motion of the club moves the golfer's head on the follow-through. This factor comes into play when the golfer observes the flight path of the ball as soon as it leaves the clubface after impact by the clubhead. The danger therein is that the golfer might neglect the club in the process and fail to complete the swinging motion of the club.

First of all, let's not forget that the **common-sense** observation of the ball before and during the swing could mean that one might think of nothing other than hitting the ball with the clubs with one's own force. The thought of swinging the club might leave or never even enter one's head in such circumstances.

Looking up to see the ball as soon as it is struck by the clubhead may be excusable with shorter clubs. A quick upward look is not too far removed from what should have been a natural reaction to the swinging motion. Furthermore, the follow-through with short clubs is quite short in itself. So the dangers of not completing the swing are not very damaging.

One is not likely to be so lucky when looking up to see the ball as soon as it is struck by the clubhead of the longer clubs, A quick, upward look in this scenario is the exact opposite from what should have been a natural reaction to the swinging motion. The natural swing of a long club moves the golfer's head horizontally since the flight path of the club on the follow-through is shallow. The movement of the head itself occurs at a slower rate since the rhythm of a longer club is slower than that of a shorter club. Furthermore, the follow-through with long clubs is significantly longer than that of shorter clubs. Thus, the dangers of not completing the swing as a consequence of looking up to see the ball's flight path prematurely are significantly increased.

Indeed, the very fact that the ball is supposed to travel greater distances with longer clubs than shorter clubs increases the naïve golfer's anxiety to observe the ball as soon as it has been impacted with the clubhead. Unfortunately, then, many errors associated with the **common sense** intention to hit the ball with the clubhead with one's own physical strength are more or less negated when employing the shorter clubs. The golfer is left confused and wondering where they are going wrong with the longer clubs.

When all is said and done, it is probably the naïve golfer's obsession with force that affects their ability to move the ball properly with every club. The naïve golfer is not concerned with *how* the clubhead contacts the ball at impact but rather with by *how much*. They may not be aware that the contact the clubhead makes with the ball at impact is as important as the force with which the clubhead impacts the ball. They may not realise that their **common sense** strategy, borne out of their life experiences and those in other ball sports, affect this seriously.

What the naïve golfer needs to understand is that the natural swinging of the golf clubs - **golf sense** - gives a greater guarantee that the appropriate amount of power can be generated to move the ball to its desired distance. It also gives a greater guarantee that the appropriate contact between ball and clubhead can occur to send it to its designated target. **Golf Sense Vs. Common Sense.**

CHANGING THE MINDSET FROM COMMON SENSE TO GOLF SENSE:

Perhaps by now, the reader can recognise whether they are "hitters" or "swingers". If you are a "hitter", then you might be better advised to re-consider your understandable and logical **common-sense** approach in moving the ball and consider a different, almost illogical logic - the swinging of the clubs for swinging sake alone - **golf sense**. One key to a successful change of mindset to the natural golf swing is to follow a series of set physical and psychological routines as described overleaf.

<u>(a) Physical Routines:</u>

You should remember that almost any kind of striking action will suffice with the shorter clubs. They do not require natural swinging motion as such and are not bound by the principles of natural swinging motion. But the middle and longer clubs do require swinging motion. The golfer should abide by the characteristics of swinging motion associated with these clubs if they attempt to create it.

The best solution is to keep the same routine that respects the characteristics of natural swinging motion with each and every club, regardless of the amount of swinging motion each club requires. What you should do, firstly, is to get into *the habit of swinging each and every club.* What you should do then is to undertake *a routine of practise-swings with the clubs* and allow your mind and body to react to and to accommodate the particular needs of the swinging motion of each club.

Thus, you are giving the clubs the amount of swinging motion they require and catering for the influences of the swinging motion on you and the ball. The reality is that once you take a practice swing or two, you do not consciously have to evaluate the needs of the swing. Your mind should be able to do so instinctively once it is not thinking about anything that might distract it from the swinging motion itself. Then you simply replicate the practise-swings for real to impact the ball since the differing physical characteristics of each swing take care of themselves once the clubs are swung naturally properly.

If you apply these routines, you can eliminate the swinging aspect of the task in moving the ball properly. If you still fail to propel the ball properly you should examine the pre-swing principles of grip and address. Surely, then, by a process of elimination and correction, you can eventually approach the task of propelling the golf ball properly with satisfaction.

Just be sure to begin the swinging motion properly. Push each clubhead back gently along the ground until it leaves the ground of its own accord. The most important part of the swing-making process is to place each clubhead into its natural flight path. Thereafter, all you have to do is sustain the swinging motion to keep the clubheads in their natural flight paths until the motion is completed.

(b) Psychological Routines: With a Relaxed Mind, the Swing is Kind:

What are even more important are mental routines to stimulate the mind to operate at levels that are conducive to creating natural swinging motion properly. Think back to the practice-sessions you have undertaken.

When your eyes were closed nothing existed for you to demonstrate abrupt, forced or aggressive physical strength/energy as you employed the clubs. There was nothing to hit the clubs with. So you actually swung the clubs naturally because there was nothing else for you to do with them. Since your mind was relaxed and not focussed on any task in particular, you could swing the clubs leisurely, rhythmically and without aggression. The other "nonsensical" exercises with the mop and the spot on the ground technique hopefully garnered similiar results.

The problem lies in the objective of the game. The dilemma, you see, is not in getting the ball into the hole. It is in getting the ball into the hole with the least amount of strokes. This is the competitive edge that focuses the golfer to think competitively. Unfortunately, any golfer who uses a somewhat unreliable method to move the ball is going to become frustrated at their efforts at stages during the competition. And this frustration inevitably leads to confrontation.

This confrontational attitude is the exact opposite of how the golfer should be thinking – in a relaxed frame of mind to swing the clubs properly. The naïve golfer approaches the task in the same determined, confrontational manner that is more suited to boxers or football players. They consequently behave in an aggressive fashion. Indeed, the reader may recall the abrupt, aggressive actions of the players in the "swing-ball" game in Chapter 2 due to their competitiveness. It is hardly likely, then, that the naïve golfer can ever create swinging motion properly since they are in an inappropriate frame of mind to do so. Indeed, the reader may recall our analogy to the dentist and the golfer going through the practise-swing checklist. Have a look at the illustration again. Notice how the golfer went to the dentist in the morning before playing golf in the afternoon? How could the golfer be relaxed on the golf course before such a frightening experience for him?

The trick, as it were, is to take the mind off the objective of the game. One should open the mind to everything and anything that distracts one from viewing golf as a competitive *task or exercise* at hand. To play the game better, you should put yourself in the right frame of mind to swing the clubs properly. This is the secret to good golf. If you play golf casually and socially with some friends then surely this is exactly why you are playing golf anyway. The reality, of course, is that very many social games of golf often have hidden competitive agendas to them. So the tendency to relax during the game is not so prevalent. If you play golf competitively, you will, of course, have to make conscious decisions regarding shot playing and so on but these factors should remain a backdrop to a relaxed mind.

You should employ some psychological strategies, then, to keep your mind relaxed during your round of golf. Just go to the golf course and do not view the round of golf as a mission to better yourself over others (saviour the victory afterwards). Leave all your worries behind you as you journey to the golf course. Make sure that you arrive there in plenty of time. When you get there, do not rush onto the first tee-box. Relax. Go to the driving range or practice area and swing some clubs first. Unwind. Go to the putting practice area. Relax. Practice a few putts. If it is a social game you are playing, try to pick a time when the course is quiet.

Even if it is a competitive game, try to suspend all your cares for the next 3/4 hours or so and view the golf course as a temporary release from all your worldly anxieties.

Put the ball on the tee-peg. Hold the club properly and address the ball properly. Concentrate on making the natural golf swing with the clubs rather than on hitting the ball with the clubs with your own force. Forget about having to put the ball into the hole with the least amount of strokes. Just swing the clubs as naturally as you can. You have come to the course to unwind and all you want to do is walk around the course. The golf ball is simply acting as your guide through the course as you go from hole to hole. Continue on from hole to hole with the same relaxed, unfocussed *golf* mentality. Enjoy the scenery. Admire the shrubbery. Exchange pleasantries with fellow players and with those that you meet. Praise and cajole your fellow players.

Do not let players ahead of you agitate you if they hold up play. Make some practice swings, observe the sky-line, engage in banter with other golfers and so on until such time as you can proceed. If a golfer or group of golfers are catching up on you, be sure that their presence behind you does not rush your behaviour on the course. You might be as well off if you let them through.

Make sure you are equipped for inclement weather. It is difficult to play golf in the rain because it affects your grip. It is also difficult to relax as you attempt to swing the clubs if you feel wet and damp. Experienced golfers carry several pairs of gloves to overcome the grip problem and several suits of wet gear to keep dry. It is hard to play golf in blustery conditions. The wind can carry the ball away and the howling of the winds can distract the relaxation of the mind. Experienced golfers wear large woolly caps over the ears to block out these howling noises. So continue your walk around the golf course. People do different things to get away from the stresses and frustrations of life. Some like casual walks; others prefer swimming; others jog, paint, do some D.I.Y.; others still take "recreational" drugs. Let the golf course become your "recreational" drug. View the course as a haven to forget about your cares for a limited period of time.

The experienced golfer knows that any mistake made comes from a poor swing. All they do is to attempt to make a better swing the next time. They forget about the bad shot and continue fresh with the next one with a relaxed approach. They have faith in the swing and they know the swing needs a relaxed mind. The naïve golfer does not know why a bad shot has arisen and is bothered by it. They become frustrated and agitated and walk straight into disaster with the following shot because the mind is still troubled and not prepared properly to swing the club naturally.

HAVE FAITH IN THE CLUBS & THE NATURAL GOLF SWING:

De-mystify the pros:

Many naive golfers are in awe of the professional golfers. There are times, of course, when the "pros" do extraordinary things on the golf course. But 99.9% of their strikes on the ball serve the principle of the swing. The "pros" may do extraordinary things but they are not, in the main, extraordinary people. They were not born with special gifts to propel the golf ball properly. The "pros", you see, are not above the laws of physics. They cannot propel the ball their way – they must observe, respect and serve the differing principles of the swing. There are exceptions, of course, who seem to use unorthodox methods of employing force onto the ball and who do so quite successfully. But golfers, in the main, abide by the natural golf swing.

The more orthodox golfers control or master the swing. They use the required energy to initiate, sustain and complete the swinging motion of each and every club. They cater for its disruptive influences by ensuring that the shoulders clear the chin and that the stance stabilises the upper body. They employ a tight finger grip on the clubs to ensure the clubheads maintain their angle of clubface throughout and impact through the ball squarely.

Yet they serve the swing. The finger grip allows the clubs to swing freely. They allow the clubhead to impact the ball. They allow the swinging motion of the clubs to influence the movement of the head on the follow-through as it should. Propelling the golf ball is a true marriage – you should give to the swing and you can take from the swing. One should be both master and servant to it. *What makes the "pros" outstanding is that they play both roles very well.* Remember - the swing is not discriminatory. The swing is available to all of us. But we, too, like the "pros" must respect and fulfil the demands of the swing.

Final words:

The vast majority of people who play golf come to the game with the appropriate physical attributes and potential to play the game well. They have two legs, two hands and a reasonable amount of agility. Yet the majority of golfers have difficulty with moving the ball with the longer clubs. Check out the statistics with the handicap secretary of your golf club or golf society. Do not be surprised to learn that 50%-75% of your fellow golfers are high-handicappers.

Why? What about all the advances in the equipment being used? What about the plethora of instruction books? Perhaps it stems from a lack of proper teaching about the golf swing? Some golf instruction books do not explain the design of the clubs and how they can function through the principle of the natural swing. Other golf instruction books do not encourage their readers to participate in practise-swinging sessions to discover the characteristics of a true golf swing for themselves so that as a result, they can understand the mistakes they are making with their present golf "swings."

Once readers understand the "complexity" of the golf swing, they can be reassured that it is, in fact, a simple physical action to recreate. The key lies in the understanding of the natural golf swing. In essence, the readers of many instructional books are not taught why the swing is everything and brought through a methodology that consequently teaches them how to swing the golf clubs naturally.

The fact is that the game of golf does not require greater physical skill levels than the majority of other ball games. It requires greater levels of particular mental skills. One should come to believe in the natural golf swing. This is what many professional golfers do. They trust the swing and adopt a few fundamentals to facilitate it. A professional will take out any club and despite how far the ball must be propelled they will believe that all they have to do is swing that club for swinging sake only. The professional has faith in the clubs – all that needs to be done is to swing them.

And come to think of it, having faith in the equipment is not uncommon in sport. Grand prix racing drivers rely on the aerodynamic design of their cars to keep the cars as close to the  ground as possible when taking corners at enormous speeds. Professional ski jumpers, for example, jump from enormous heights and travel through the air at over 90 km per hour. Yet, they do very little as they sail through the air. Once they have tilted their bodies to become parallel with the skis, they simply stare ahead into the horizon. They keep their head still. They keep their arms rigid. They keep their legs braced. Just like good golfers do. Essentially, once in flight, they do nothing at all yet fly gracefully until they approach the down-slope when they must adjust their bodies for a suitable landing. These people put their lives on the line yet they stare into space and keep their bodies as still as possible as they hurtle through the air. Why? Because they have faith in the skis. Just like good golfers have faith in the clubs and the natural swing. It's all in the mind.

175

Take out the cleaning mop you swung earlier in Chapter 3. Grip it correctly and swing it with the eyes closed. Can you discern the smoothness and fluidity of the motions the mop takes as it revolves around your body? Can you sense the power such motions could create? Can you discern how these motions could move your head on the follow-through? This is the natural swinging motion of a mop. No golf ball or golf target exists. Wasn't this natural swinging motion easy to create in such circumstances?

Now you are ready - off you go to your golf course and employ all of your golf clubs in the same manner. Be wary of using your **common sense** to hit the ball with the clubs with your own force. Try instead to use some **golf sense** and swing the clubs naturally. But the circumstances have changed since a golf ball and target now come into play. Will these distract you from creating natural swinging motion with the clubs? Or will you now show the mental strength to trust the clubs and the concept of the natural swing? I hope you show the latter. JUST SWING THE CLUBS FOR SWINGING SAKE ONLY AND LET THEM DO THE WORK! Good luck!!